A Frontier Texas Mercantile:

The History of Gibbs Brothers and Company, Huntsville, 1841-1940

A Frontier Texas Mercantile:

The History of Gibbs Brothers and Company, Huntsville, 1841-1940

By

Donald R. Walker

Texas Review Press
Huntsville, Texas

Printed in the United States of America

FIRST EDITION, 1997

Library of Congress Cataloging-in-Publication Data

Walker, Donald R. (Donald Roy), 1941-
A frontier Texas mercantile: the history of Gibbs Brothers and Company, Huntsville, 1841-1940 / by Donald R. Walker.
p. cm.
Includes bibliographical references and index.
ISBN 1-881515-08-7 (hc)
1. Gibbs Brothers and Company—History. 2. General stores—Texas—Huntsville—History. 3. Gibbs family. I. Title.
HF5429.5.H86W35 1997
381'. 1'09764'69—dc21 96-47120
CIP

Cover design by Paul Ruffin and Mary Laura Gibbs. On the front cover is a photograph of the first page of Ledger B (courtesy of Gibbs Brothers and Company), filled out Saturday evening, September 4, 1841, upon the arrival of Gibbs and Coffin in Huntsville. On the back cover is a photograph of the earliest known sketch of Huntsville (circa 1843), from *William Bollarert's Texas*, reprinted courtesy of the Walker County Historical Commission and the Office of Library Services, Newberry Library (Chicago).

This book is dedicated

to the life and memory of

Wilbourn Sandford Gibbs,
1909-1982

A Frontier Texas Mercantile:

The History of Gibbs Brothers and Company, Huntsville, 1841-1940

PREFACE AND ACKNOWLEDGEMENTS

On a sunny January day in 1964, a representative from the Texas State Historical Commission travelled to Huntsville to make a presentation. In the award, the firm of Gibbs Brothers and Company was designated the "oldest . . . in Texas under original ownership and on [the] first site." Founded when Texas was still a republic, Gibbs Brothers has, through the years, engaged in the mercantile business, in banking, and in the successful management of vast holdings in land, timber, and mineral resources. Throughout it all, the company headquarters has remained at the original location on the courthouse square in Huntsville.[1]

Regrettably, the members of the historical commission undertook no extensive search of state or local records before making the award to the Gibbs family. Thus, others may challenge and claim to be the oldest in the state. But whether Gibbs Brothers is indeed the senior firm in Texas is a matter of relatively minor importance. The uninterrupted history of the company, stretching back for more than a century and a half, distinguishes it beyond the necessity for verification by the state commission.[2]

Chances are, if one were to stop at random a pedestrian on any street in any Texas city, save Huntsville, and ask if he or she had heard of Gibbs Brothers and Company, the response would be negative. In part, this can be explained by the presence in contemporary Texas cities of large numbers of people who were born and raised elsewhere and have only recently settled in the Lone Star State. More importantly, however, it stems from the fact that the company does not seek public recognition. Gibbs Brothers manufactures nothing for sale directly to the public so has no need for advertising, or public relations campaigns, to spread the company name. There have been periodic newspaper stories and other journalistic treatments of various aspects of the company's history and operations, but these have been rare and marked by a lack of significant detail, occasioned, no doubt, by the rigid space limitations that prevail in the newspaper business. Moreover, most writing about the company—some of it quite informative—has appeared only in local publications that have not enjoyed broad dissemination outside the immediate Walker County area. For all these reasons, few people are aware of Gibbs Brothers or have any understanding of its significance in the economic life of the greater Southeast Texas area. This study seeks to correct the lack of information, and the abundance of misinformation, that prevail about the company.

During the course of the research and writing of this manuscript, the author has profited from the observations and perspectives of others who have investigated similar businesses in other parts of the country. Careful reading of these earlier works provided insights essential to developing a framework within which to view both the growth of Gibbs Brothers and the role it played in helping to transform the economy of East Texas from one of primitive local subsistence to regional cooperation in the carefully-monitored utilization of both renewable and non-renewable resources.

One of the first scholarly treatments of the role of businessmen in the development of frontier societies in the United States appeared in 1939. Lewis E. Atherton, in *The Pioneer Merchant in Mid-America*, credits the early commercial classes with having exerted a profound stabilizing influence in the small villages on the western edge of settlement. The small store owners customarily engaged in banking, land development, farming, and incipient local manufacturing, in addition to the retailing of goods and merchandise. The products available in the frontier general mercantiles helped raise the standard of living in the local area from one of minimal survival to another in which economic specialization and the development of trades and professions could proceed. Moreover, the items carried in the stores' inventories re-established the link with the older towns and communities back East from whence most of the local townspeople had come, thereby enabling the diffusion of social and cultural advances westward.[3]

A few years later, in *The Southern Country Store, 1800-1860*, Atherton focused his attention on the rural general store and the important position it occupied in the economic life of the antebellum South. He confirmed his findings made earlier in his work in the Midwest and went on to note that Southern rural merchants frequently represented the only source of capital in a rural area. Additionally, they generally had the only regular contacts with economic and financial interests outside the region, thus giving them further control over the movement of goods and products in and out of a region.[4]

Researching in the same general subject area, Thomas D. Clark, in *Pills, Petticoats, and Plows: The Southern Country Store*, confirmed most of Atherton's findings, especially those that argued the vital role played by storeowners in leading the economic growth in their towns. Drawing on a wealth of records from small businesses throughout the Deep South, Clark demonstrated the fundamental importance of the general store to community life. The variety of merchandise offered for sale attracted interest from all segments of local society, with the result that the stores became gathering places where local citizens would congregate to discuss recent news, crop prospects for the year, and other matters of local interest. Most of the stores also functioned as post offices as well as the sources for local and out-of-town newspapers, thus providing a further attraction to all who came to town.[5]

In perhaps his most surprising observation, Clark found that, contrary to prevailing and long-held beliefs, most Southern storeowners were honest and forthright in their business dealings. Ledger entries, for example, showing that customers had been cheated in a particular transaction were offset by others in which the owners had defrauded themselves. Clark contended that both types of situations resulted from legitimate errors in tabulation and bookkeeping rather than from deliberate attempts by the storeowners to take unfair advantage of customers and plunder the local economy for their own benefit.[6]

Other works that have proven especially useful include *The Road to Spindletop: Economic Change in Texas, 1875-1901*, by

John Stricklin Spratt and *A Financial History of Texas*, by Edmund Miller. Both of these books, while badly in need of updating, were helpful in providing a general picture of economic changes as the state matured and entered the modern era.[7] A more extensive listing of sources consulted can be found in the bibliography at the end of the book.

The history of Gibbs Brothers that follows will consist of a detailed look at every aspect of the development of the company from its founding as a general mercantile store in 1841 through the Depression years of the 1930's. The decision to terminate the history at that point arose from the realization that to bring it any closer to the present might require the release of information that could prove prejudicial to current company operations. Moreover, since by that time virtually all elements of the modern firm and its activities had fully emerged and were well-established, any discussion of matters beyond that date would have added little of substance to the story. A further limitation will be found in the absence of any disclosures concerning individual members of the Gibbs family. With the exception of Thomas and Sandford St. John Gibbs and their spouses; no information of a personal or financial nature regarding any Gibbs descendants will be discussed. In part, the decision to omit information on individual family members was made in the belief that such revelations were not germane to the story of the company. Furthermore, a detailed probe into the personal lives of individual family members would have constituted an unnecessary invasion of their privacy.

To a significant degree, the history of Gibbs Brothers and Company forms a mirror from which one may view the economic history of the entire state and region, with a particular emphasis on the development of greater Southeast Texas. Having been in continuous operation for so many years, Gibbs Brothers has prospered along with everyone else during good times and suffered along with them in adversity. The company has participated in the development of new industries to provide employment to area workers, has promoted the wise and efficient use of natural resources, and has used its assets and influence to help establish recreational areas that are of benefit to all citizens in the region.

Until the very recent past, most of the Gibbs family members lived in or near Huntsville and identified closely with the town and with Walker County. Unlike absentee owners, they managed their resources and assets with the well-being of the local area firmly in mind. Gibbs children grew up in Huntsville, were educated in the Huntsville public schools, and participated in the various activities for youth available in the community. As adults, they fulfilled their community responsibilities by providing financial support, encouragement, and leadership for civic clubs, educational and religious organizations, and the several local chambers of commerce and industry.

The modern Gibbs Brothers and Company clearly predominates as the most important center of economic power in Walker County. Although other families have been in the county longer, and at one time were wealthier and owned more land, only Gibbs Brothers has managed to expand its holdings and increase its assets despite the reverses and misfortunes associated with economic downturns and recessions. The reasons for the success of the company will be explored fully in the history that follows. An examination will be made of the founding of the company, the various periods through which it has passed, the kinds of policies it has pursued through the years, the types of business activities in which it has engaged, and the success it has enjoyed. Most importantly, the history will focus sharply on the evolution of the company leadership and the degree to which the firm today continues to follow the keen, astute precepts and practices first enunciated and put into force well over a century ago by Thomas and Sandford Gibbs.

In preparing this manuscript, the author was the recipient of many courtesies and incurred a number of debts that must be acknowledged. To Wilbourn Sandford Gibbs must go the credit for having conceived the idea of a company history. Through much of his adult life, Gibbs assiduously collected bits of company and family history and kept them together so that they could be used by later researchers and authors, as well as younger members of the family interested in the firm. Gibbs took great pride in Huntsville and its citizens and believed strongly that, having been born into a position of great privilege, he had acquired great responsibilities to use his influence to improve conditions around him. His death in 1982 was truly a loss for the progressive elements in Walker County.

Ruth Farrington Gibbs, widow of Wilbourn Sandford Gibbs, shared her former husband's historical interests and generously supported the costs of the research and writing. The members of the extended Gibbs family, as well as everyone with an appreciation for Texas history, owe these two persons a tremendous debt for their foresight in recognizing the value of a company history and their willingness to assume the responsibility of having the story told.

Judge Thomas Gibbs Gee, who served as senior partner of Gibbs Brothers during the time of the research, continued the commitment to see the company story in print. Judge Gee has uniformly supported and encouraged the history. In addition to his legal talent, he is also a writer of considerable ability and has stimulated me to bring to this work as much precision and accuracy as possible.

Virginia Gibbs Smyth and Sarah Hawley Potter, granddaughters of Sandford and Sallie Gibbs, made available to me their many insights into the family history. Both remember a great many of the stories, both fact and fancy, that have circulated about the Gibbs family through the years and were able to provide detail for and confirmation of those that could be used in the construction of this narrative. Mary Laura Gibbs, great-granddaughter of Sandford and Sallie, read the first draft of the manuscript thoroughly and provided a number of helpful suggestions to be incorporated into the final copy.

Thanks also must go to the employees of Gibbs Brothers and Company, those persons most intimately responsible for the day-to-day operations of the company. Messrs. Tom Randle, Ed Sandhop, Jr., and Raymond Carroll gave generously and willingly of their time and expertise and were unfailingly courteous and patient in answering my questions, even as I disrupted their schedules and activities by roaming through the company vaults poring over old records and correspondence. Ferne Frosch and Diane Cotten assisted by relating to me their knowledge of the company and by ensuring that I had a quiet place to work. Rhonda Ernst shared with me her understanding and knowledge of Gibbs Brothers land transactions and spent a good bit of her time sitting in the Walker County Courthouse carefully gleaning information from antiquated, and barely-legible, tax rolls and court records. To W.L. (Bill) Carroll, I wish to express my thanks for relating to me his immense store of information on Gibbs Brothers lumbering practices. Carroll spent nearly a half-century as a Gibbs employee and, as an experienced forester thoroughly familiar with all aspects of the business, he was able to explain to me in very clear and succinct terms the pertinent details of the Gibbs operation and the rationale behind the evolution of the company's timber management policies. All of these people contributed immensely to whatever quality this manuscript possesses and all are due a large measure of gratitude.

A special mention of appreciation must also go to Professor Charles Dwyer, former director of the Thomason Rare Books Room at Sam Houston State University, and to Mary Vick Rainey of the Sam Houston State University Archives. Professor Dwyer, although not a native of Huntsville, spent a good many years there associated with the university library. His wide reading in the historical materials covering both Texas and Walker County, as well as his perceptive understanding of local institutions and personalities, enabled him to guide me through some particularly confusing periods in the Gibbs story. It is seldom that one meets a true bibliophile, like Charles Dwyer, who combines a keen love of books with a profound comprehension of their contents. His recent retirement constitutes a substantial loss to the entire university community. Mary Rainey, a lifelong resident of Walker County and a member of one of the older families in the area, is also an avid student of local history and was able to direct me to many sources that I might otherwise have overlooked. Her knowledge of Walker County history is equalled by few, and the pleasant, helpful attitude she brings to her work makes her a most valuable asset to any researcher.

Acknowledgement must also be made of the assistance and advice given by Alwyn Barr, Paul Carlson, and Joseph E. King of the Texas Tech University history department. All of these individuals gave willingly of their time and expertise and suggested fruitful areas of research. In addition, they read the finished manuscript and made a number of suggestions to clarify particular points and polish the final product.

And finally, as in all things, I must acknowledge the tremendous debt I owe to members of my family. My parents, Gaus W. Walker, Jr., and Juanita Sellars Walker, gentle and decent people, instilled in me a respect for learning and scholarship that continues to be the most gratifying and rewarding legacy anyone could ever receive. My wife, Jonette, and my daughters, Jolie and Jennie, gave unstintingly of their patience, understanding, and encouragement throughout the time required for the research and the writing of the Gibbs story. I shall be in their debt always.

Contents

INTRODUCTION

In a windshield tour of Texas, published in 1940 by the state highway department and the Works Project Administration, an unknown author described Huntsville as a "dignified old town." The community "spreads over red sandy hills, from the top of one of which the grim gray towers of the Texas State Penitentiary frown down . . . ."[1] While such a description might have been an accurate impression of what the wartime visitor saw, most Huntsville citizens likely would have objected to the morbid suggestion that their town existed under the foreboding presence of the prison. Most Huntsville residents would have preferred to think of their city as a pleasant, respectable, fundamentally conservative place where, by dint of thrift and hard work, one could hope to enjoy all the finer benefits of life in a small town. They would have agreed with an earlier writer who pictured Huntsville as "a place that has never known a boom, never made haste to get rich, or sought to captivate the populace by rainbow-tinted promises, fictitious values or ostentatious boasts."[2] In short, a nice place to live and raise a family.

To the modern visitor, Huntsville appears to be something of a study in contrasts. The charm, grace, and dignity of some of the older buildings and residences in town bespeak a gentle and genteel past, while the fast food restaurants and national chain store outlets that have sprung up along the interstate highway bear witness to the arrival of impersonal contemporary commercial methods and foreshadow the inevitable, and regrettable, invasion of the architectural shabbiness and impermanence of modern society. Thus far, Huntsville has managed to maintain a distinct urban identity, despite the enormous pressures to homogenize American cities and make them all look the same. There is a recognizable, thriving downtown area, with small shops and stores clustered around the courthouse square, and local merchants have undertaken beautification and revitalization campaigns to preserve the integrity and vibrancy of the historic commercial district. The people in Huntsville still greet each other and stop to talk when they meet on the street, and a feeling of tranquillity envelops the visitor as he makes his way about the town. One likes to think that were the founders of the town to return today to visit, they would be impressed with the progress and development that have come over the years and would be pleased that a distinct flavor of the past has been preserved.

The history of Huntsville stretches back to the earliest years of Anglo-American settlement in Texas. In 1834, Pleasant Gray, who hailed from Alabama, petitioned the Government of Mexico for permission to establish a settlement in what was then the Mexican province of Coahuila and Texas. The request was approved in July of 1835 and shortly thereafter Gray built a crude residence for his family on the eastern edge of a small prairie, much of which is now taken up by the courthouse square. At the same time, he constructed a trading post that would serve the needs of the peaceful Indians living nearby, as well as the immigrants coming into the area from the United States. As Gray's settlement grew and began to take on the appearance of an established community, he christened it "Huntsville" in honor of his former home in Alabama.[3]

The site Gray selected for his town had much to offer its early inhabitants. Located amidst gently rolling hills with moderate year-round temperatures and ample rainfall, Huntsville could promise its residents an abundance of wild game and fish in the dense nearby forests and the several rivers and streams that coursed through the area. The broad expanses of fertile prairie portended the establishment of prosperous farms whose owners would promote political stability for the region and provide a solid foundation for steady economic growth. The absence of good all-weather roads into the area, so essential to commercial success, was overcome by the presence of the Trinity River a few miles to the east of town. River travel promised excellent communications with the towns along the Gulf Coast as well as with new settlements, like Crockett and

Palestine, that were beginning to spring up along the river to the north. The only serious question to trouble the new settlers lay in the deteriorating political relations between the American-born residents in the area and the national government in Mexico City.

By the mid-1830's, the northern reaches of Coahuila and Texas had begun to feel the effects of the intense political divisions and resulting factional fighting that had characterized political life in the Mexican capital since the late 1820's. The bitter struggles between the Centralists, those who wanted to concentrate more power in the central government, and the Federalists, who wished more autonomy to reside at the state level, had paralyzed the Mexican political machinery to the point that little or no effective governing could take place. Such inactivity greatly concerned many of the residents in the eastern Texas area who looked to the Mexican government to settle particularly urgent matters involving immigration, the administration of justice in accordance with democratic principles, and the guaranteeing of land titles. The Mexican government, for its part, suspected that the discontent and unrest in eastern Coahuila and Texas represented little more than the surface manifestation of a much deeper desire on the part of the local residents to break away from Mexico and form a separate government.[4]

The principal underlying cause of the growing estrangement between the Mexican government and its American subjects lay in the profound cultural and political differences that animated both sides. The Anglo-Americans, whose political traditions included respect for individual freedoms and the guarantees of legal recourse to redress grievances, had difficulty adjusting to life under a government that, although nominally democratic and free of colonial control, continued to draw from the elitist and authoritarian experiences of Spanish rule. A stark example of the unpleasant reality facing the Mexicans came in 1828, when an expedition from Mexico City sent to assess the eastern Texas situation reported its findings. The expedition commander, General Manuel Mier y Teran, a respected military officer and hero of the Mexican Revolution to break away from Spain, reported that as one entered eastern Texas, the Mexican influence diminished quickly:

> The whole population here is a mixture of strange and incoherent parts without parallel in our federation; numerous tribes of Indians, now at peace, but armed and at any moment ready for war, whose steps toward civilization should be taken under the close supervision of a strong and intelligent government; colonists [Americans] of another people, more progressive and better informed than the Mexican inhabitants, but also more shrewd and unruly; among these foreigners are fugitives from justice, honest laborers, vagabonds and criminals, but honorable and dishonorable alike travel with their political constitution in their pockets, demanding privileges, authority and officers which such a constitution guarantees.[5]

Confusion, suspicion, and mistrust on both sides ultimately resulted in a determination by the Mexican president, General Antonio Lopez de Santa Anna, to take military action to bring the Americans into line and an equally fervent resolve on the part of the Americans to resist what they perceived as military coercion. The ensuing course of events led to a Texas declaration of independence from Mexico in early March, 1836, a declaration ratified and made permanent by the defeat of the Mexican army at San Jacinto on the afternoon of April 21, 1836.[6]

The defeat of the Mexican army ushered in a period of almost ten years when Texas existed somewhat precariously as an independent republic. The new government had to concern itself with ongoing problems of defense from possible attacks by Mexico, anxious to regain lost territory, and from Native Americans, whom the Texans did not trust to remain docile and peaceful. Coupled with this was the necessity of trying to establish the government on a sound financial footing and providing those basic services that one expects of a legally-constituted political authority. It was during this republic period, when the continued existence of an independent Texas was far from confirmed, that Thomas Gibbs arrived in Huntsville, established his business, and irrevocably linked his future and fortune with that of the new country.

The Gibbs lineage represented by Thomas and his brother Sandford, who joined the business in 1847, descended from James Gibbs, a prominent South Carolinian, who had established himself and his family in Union District well before the American Revolution. Little is known about James apart from the fact that he fought on the American side during the Revolutionary War and likely earned his living as a farmer. He married Anne Barnett Johnson, from Orange County, Virginia, on July 8, 1771, and she bore him eight children, five sons and three daughters. One of the sons, Hiram, born on August 30, 1785, eventually moved out of the South Carolina area and headed westward to Mississippi, one of the newer states of the South. Before leaving, however, he married Sabra Ann Wilbourne and fathered eight children. Thomas, the second child of Hiram and Sabra Ann, planted the family's roots firmly in Walker County, Texas.[7]

In 1847 in Huntsville, Thomas married Nancy Theresa Rogers, forging a union that produced one child, Minerva Anne. Nancy died in August, 1856, and three years later Thomas married Mary Sophia Blake. The second marriage produced seven children, five of whom reached maturity. Sandford St. John Gibbs, the sixth child of Hiram and Sabra Ann, was born on July 7, 1819. On March 14, 1855, he married Mary Wilmuth Gary, who presented him with one child, Lena, born in 1857. Mary died in January, 1863, and three years later Sandford married Sallie E. Smith, of Plantersville, Texas. The marriage of Sandford and Sallie Smith Gibbs endured until Sandford's death in 1886 and produced six children.[8] The history that follows will chronicle the activities of the Thomas and Sandford Gibbs families and their role in pioneering the settlement and development of Walker County and the greater Southeast Texas area.

A Frontier Texas Mercantile:

The History of Gibbs Brothers and Company, Huntsville, 1841-1940

—I—

The First Half Century, 1841-1886

Thomas Gibbs, the first of his family to make his home in Huntsville, arrived in Pleasant Gray's new settlement late on the afternoon of Saturday, September 4, 1841. He and his business partner, Gardner R. Coffin, immediately broke out the load of supplies and goods they had brought with them into Texas and opened their business. Apart from the place and date of his birth, little is known of Thomas Gibbs's activities prior to his arrival in Texas, and details surrounding the early life of Gardner Coffin are even more obscure. Indeed, we have no idea where, or when, the two men met and how they came to decide to go into business together. Coffin's father lived in New York state, so it is reasonable to assume that the younger Coffin was also a New Yorker. Family records assert that Thomas Gibbs engaged briefly in the mercantile business in Louisiana and Mississippi after leaving his home state of South Carolina, but the circumstances that brought the two men to Texas remain a mystery.[1]

The migration of Gibbs and Coffin westward through the Deep South, carrying a limited stock of goods, identifies them as members of a much larger group of itinerant merchants who followed similar paths and trails during the antebellum period and formed a significant element "in the merchandising world of the South." Leaving homes and friends behind, these nomadic traders pushed into areas as yet unsettled, except for a scattered few hardy souls. When prospects for economic development and town growth in a particular area seemed good, the travellers would cease their wanderings and settle down to become prosperous storekeepers and community boosters.[2]

The few bits of information that describe the land and people of Texas in the mid-nineteenth century when Gibbs and Coffin arrived focus almost exclusively on the economic potential of the region rather than on any accomplished growth or development. The most common sources available are in the form of diaries, or daily logs, of persons from the United States who, for any of a variety of reasons, had occasion to visit the new republic. Most commented favorably on Texas, but all noted the relatively primitive conditions under which people lived, especially in areas like East Texas that were situated at some distance from the older established towns along the coast or near the rivers in the central part of the region. Mary Austin Holley, cousin of Stephen F. Austin, wrote one of the earliest accounts. Holley made her trip to Texas in the early 1830's, a few years before the revolution to break away from Mexico. She came at the invitation of Austin, who offered her a league of land, 4,428 acres, if she would settle and make her home in his colony. Holley never resided in Texas but wrote two books about the new territory, both designed to present as favorable a picture as possible of the land in which her cousin had invested so much of his time and effort.[3]

Holley presented Texas as a country of three distinct topographical regions, which she termed level, undulating, and mountainous. The level region consisted of "the entire coast, extending from 30 to 80 miles into the interior." It was "destitute of timber, except narrow skirts on the margin of rivers and creeks."

> Its distinguishing and happy peculiarity is, that, although rather low, and so extremely level, that the scope of the eye comprises a horizon of many miles, it is entirely free of marsh; so much so, that, in most places, a loaded wagon may be driven to the beach without obstruction.[4]

North of the level region, one encountered the undulating parts of Texas. These, although "more-elevated" than the level portions, and "presenting a perpetually varying surface," never broke into sharp ridges or elevations that could be called hilly or mountainous.

The changes in the terrain were more gradual than abrupt, or steep, such as would characterize hills and mountains. The undulating region above the upper Texas coast, and which included the area around Huntsville, was composed of dense forests that were drained by several large rivers, "which afford many favorable sites for saw-mills and manufactories": It is "heavily timbered with pine, oak, ash, cedar, cypress, and other forest trees, which extend [to the] Red river [*sic*], occasionally variegated by small prairies containing from one hundred to one thousand acres." The soil was well suited for "grazing and agriculture," and, in Holley's view, the "timber business will be extensive and lucrative in this section."[5]

As for the mountainous region, which lay to the north and west of the undulating areas, Holley pronounced it "of vast advantage" to the rest of Texas:

> It not only renders the atmosphere more salubrious but, abounding in copious fountains of limpid water, it gives rise to the numerous rivulets which, having first irrigated their own fruitful vallies, flow off with a rapid current, and unite to form the large rivers . . . of the State.[6]

Holley also wrote of the principal towns in Texas (Huntsville was not among them), but cautioned her readers against thinking in terms of well-established communities, such as one might expect to find in the older sections of the United States.

> In a country so recently settled as Texas one must not look for large and populous towns and cities. Every man who purchases a large plantation . . . immediately lays out [a town]. Hence, a vast number of nominal towns are, in reality, not even villages; sometimes containing not more than a dwelling or two . . . . The most populous settlements, even, are as yet small places . . . .

The principal reason for the lack of urbanization lay in the vastness of Texas and the scarcity of people living there: "Population is, as yet, sparse, widely-scattered, and of a very roving character; and, consequently . . . the future destinies of towns . . . are involved in much doubt . . . ."[7]

A decade or so after Holley's sojourn in Texas, two English visitors, E.M. Houstoun and wife, arrived to write a series of articles for the *London News*. The dispatches were later collected and published in book form. Like Mary Holley before them, the Houstouns were favorably impressed with the climate and topography of Texas and also had complimentary remarks to make on the industry and hospitality of those Texans living in the coastal cities. Owing to a lack of good roads, the Houstouns did not travel very far inland from Galveston, where they had entered the republic, but did manage to make a few trips into the interior just across Galveston Bay. They remarked on the amazing abundance and variety of both wild and domesticated animal life and reasoned that an individual could live very well amidst such bounty with little personal effort or sacrifice. The few negative comments made by the two Britishers came when they spoke of the large numbers of feral pigs that roamed everywhere, even in city streets. The animals presented such a disgustingly filthy appearance and fed on such a frightful assortment of carrion and other wastes that the Houstouns dreaded even seeing them and vowed not to eat pork as long as they remained in Texas. Further criticisms came when the writers discussed the problems that prevailed in getting clear title to land one might wish to purchase. The Houstouns quoted some of the more prominent attorneys who argued (perhaps in their own interest) that "the titles to three-fourths of the . . . lands in Texas were of a doubtful character; not perhaps absolutely invalid, but admitting of a lawsuit [to resolve]." The problems arose from the nature of the land titles conferred by the Mexican government and those awarded later by the Republic of Texas. Many of the former had contained certain specific provisions that had not been met by the grantees, or impresarios, so, technically, were invalid. But the grantees had proceeded to establish settlements regardless and would not yield control of the land willingly. The titles conferred by the Texas government were not much better as they appeared "to have been granted so incautiously, and to have offered at the same time so many facilities for fraud and deception that at present it is almost impossible to pronounce any particular one of these titles to be good or bad . . . ." The Houstouns refrained from discouraging immigration and settlement in Texas, however, saying that clear titles to land could be obtained if one were diligent and patient in checking any potential counterclaims or discrepancies and that such an effort was well worth taking as land was much cheaper in the new republic than it was in either Europe or the United States.[8]

A third source one may check for observations on life in Texas during the middle 1800's is that of Frederick Law Olmsted, a journalist and landscape architect from New York, who made a four-month visit to the new state in the early 1850's. Accompanied by his brother, Olmsted entered Texas at a point somewhere between Natchitoches, Louisiana, and San Augustine, Texas, and described a typical dwelling in the area, which he termed a "Red River Plantation":

> The house was a small square log cabin, with a broad open shed or piazza in front, and a chimney, made of sticks and mud, leaning against one end. A smaller detached cabin, twenty feet in the rear, was used for a kitchen. A cistern under a roof, and collecting water from three roofs, stood between. The water from the [nearby] bayou was not fit to drink, nor is the water of . . . any springs in this region. The people depend entirely on cisterns for drinking water. It's very little white folks need, however—milk, claret, and whisky being the more common beverages.

Asked for something to eat, the lady of the plantation served the travellers a meal which, much to their regret, proved to be the standard fare throughout East Texas. They were offered "a plate of cold, salt, fat pork; a cup of what to both eye and tongue seemed lard, but which she termed butter; a plate of very stale, dry, flaky, micaceous corn-bread; a jug of molasses, and a pitcher of milk." The men found they had no stomach for anything but the milk. The Olmsteds were further dismayed to observe that no one they encountered in East Texas demonstrated any interest in reading or had any particular understanding of national or world events. It was as if the area existed in a state of self-imposed isolation from the world around it. Houses were generally poorly built and poorly maintained so that they tended toward dilapidation; livestock herds roamed about freely with little attention or care from their owners, and, with the exception of the women, the people one encountered were crude and given to excessive cursing, swearing, and indolence. Olmsted blamed the blighted condition of East Texas on the institution of slavery, which he believed to exert a pernicious and destructive effect on whites in that it bred a contempt for civility and hard work among the slaveowners. The two brothers saw a good bit of East Texas between Centerville to the north and Beaumont to the south. They did not visit Huntsville, but their comments of neighboring areas strongly suggest that had they ventured into Walker County they would not have found conditions much different from those elsewhere in the region.[9]

The generally underdeveloped nature of much of East Texas and its people during the mid-nineteenth century may explain, in part at least, the success Gibbs and Coffin enjoyed in their business operations. The careful and professional manner with which they took care of all their commercial transactions indicates clearly that the two men brought with them to Huntsville considerable experience, plus a familiarity with business methods practiced elsewhere in the United States where economic and financial development had proceeded much further. In an area like East Texas, where educational levels were fairly low, where there was little concern for formal learning and much ignorance of the outside world, their keen sense of how to protect and enhance their interests would have helped immeasurably as they planned for the future and expanded their operation.

A further advantage held by the two men lay in the financial resources that supported their business venture through the critical early years. All previous accounts of the founding of the store have mentioned that Gibbs and Coffin arrived in Huntsville with a small stock of goods upon which to stake their future. And, indeed, the two men may have had little merchandise with them on the occasion of their initial arrival in Walker County. Such would have been in keeping with the "itinerant" nature of their business before arriving in Texas. But the rapidity with which they acquired substantial holdings in real estate once they established themselves in Walker County, as well as the size of their cash reserves, establishes that they had considerable capital they could call upon if needed. The money likely came either from profits of business ventures they had undertaken earlier as they made their way across the South, or from family inheritances.

Upon their arrival in Huntsville, Gibbs and Coffin rented space for their business from Thomas G. Bailey, who charged them $5.00 per month. They boarded with F. B. Pankey for a charge of $12 per month. Pankey also provided laundry service for the two men, both of whom were single, for an extra fee. These arrangements proved to be only temporary, however, and by early 1842 the firm of Gibbs and Coffin had moved and begun renting its store space from Pleasant Gray, who charged them at the same rate as had Bailey. Also in the early months of 1842, the two men began boarding with Sherman Drury, who charged them 33 cents per day. John Kennan provided laundry service for the two at the rate of $1.25 per month. By the middle of 1842, Gibbs and Coffin found themselves firmly established in business and in a position to begin making permanent investments in their new hometown, and opportunities for such began to appear rather quickly.[10]

During the latter months of 1841 and early 1842, Pleasant Gray bought a substantial quantity of merchandise from Gibbs and Coffin on credit, an indication, perhaps, that Gray's trading post either had ceased to function or carried a very limited variety of goods. During the spring of 1842, Gray signed a promissory note to cover the $83.26 in purchases he had made at Gibbs and Coffin since September, 1841. The note was to fall due in sixty days. By July, 1842, Gray had charged merchandise totalling an additional $100, and he took care of this latter indebtedness by signing a single, larger note that covered everything he owed the two men. The parties agreed that the second obligation would be due for payment anytime between May and November, 1843. Gray put up the store rented by Gibbs and Coffin and the adjacent lot used by the company as collateral. For some reason, however, Gray did not let the note go to maturity. On October 11, 1842 he deeded to Gibbs and Coffin the store and adjacent lot and they cancelled all his indebtedness to them, which, by that time, had reached $192.91. The deed transferring the property from Pleasant Gray to the two businessmen contained the following description of the land:

> [The] south part of Lot #3, in block # 1, fronting on Cedar Street [11th Street], beginning at the southwest corner of said lot, thence due North with western boundary of said lot a distance of 75 feet; thence due East 75 feet to eastern boundary of said lot; thence due South 75 feet to southeast corner of said lot; thence due West a distance of 75 feet to the beginning corner.

The selling price came to $300, which meant that Gibbs and Coffin paid Gray $107.09, that is, the difference between the price of the property and Gray's indebtedness to them. Thus, by the end of their first year of operation, Gibbs and Coffin had a permanent location for their firm and business seemed to be going well.[11]

Unfortunately, at about that same time, a serious problem arose and cast grave doubts as to the future of the business. By late 1842, Coffin's health had begun to decline. The nature of his illness remains a mystery, but by the end of that year he was "too low to be able to attend to business matters." Sensing, perhaps, the seriousness of his condition, Coffin hired John McCreary, a regular customer in the store, to put in writing all of the agreements and arrangements he had entered into with Thomas Gibbs. And within a few months of the new year, 1843, Coffin was dead. Shortly after the demise of his partner, Thomas Gibbs settled all business matters with Coffin's father, Nathan, who travelled to Huntsville to see the business his son had helped establish. In the final settlement, reached in 1844, an appraisal was made of the store and all merchandise owned jointly by the former partners. The appraiser reckoned the total value to be $150. Nathan Coffin accepted this figure and Gibbs paid $75 for Gardner Coffin's interest, thereby taking over sole ownership of the firm. He continued to operate the business by himself until January, 1847, when his younger brother, Sandford St. John Gibbs, arrived in Huntsville and paid $500 for a one-half interest in the firm. The name of the company was changed to "T. & S. Gibbs" to reflect the nature of the dual ownership, but company operations remained essentially the same as had been the case when Coffin was a partner.[12]

The apparent discrepancy between the appraised value of the store, plus inventory, and the price paid earlier to Gray by Gibbs and

Coffin raises questions as to why the figures do not coincide, or at least, more nearly approximate each other; unfortunately, none of the evidence available provides conclusive answers. Among the possible explanations: (1) the store, with inventory, and the lot in Huntsville may, indeed, have been worth only $150 as the appraiser figured. That is, Gibbs and Coffin may have paid Pleasant Gray too much for the property they bought; or (2) Gibbs and Coffin may not have been equal partners in their business. Gibbs may have invested more of his resources in the firm so that the amount of property owned equally would have totalled only $150; or (3) Thomas Gibbs may have provided other compensation, in addition to money, to the elder Coffin for his son's interest in the business, and there is evidence to indicate that this may have been the case. A check of the tax rolls for Walker County in 1846 reveals that among his other possessions, Gibbs listed 1,000 acres (valued at $500) in Harris County for which he served as principal agent for Nathan Coffin, the owner of the land. Gibbs may have agreed to look after the land for Coffin (who had returned to New York) and help find a buyer for it as part of the final settlement between the two men.[13]

The general mercantile founded by Gibbs and Coffin and operated later by the two Gibbs brothers was typical of a great many similar establishments throughout the rural South. It offered a variety of different types of goods, but with only a limited selection of any particular item. That is to say, the store carried many different categories of things, but with few choices as to style, color, or design within the different categories. Gibbses' customers could buy everything from food to clothing to agricultural implements to cooking utensils to medicines, with a concentration in those items that could not be produced easily on the small farms on which most store patrons lived. Foodstuffs sold in the store were primarily staple items, such as flour, salt, sugar, cornmeal, coffee, and spices, with fresh fruits in season. The store also handled small inventories of packaged foods, like canned crackers, and processed items, such as smoked meats and dried fish, but these were more expensive and sales of them remained relatively small. The clothing, shoes, and fabric carried in the store tended to be of the more durable variety, although higher quality luxury items could be obtained through special order. Shoes, for example, were usually the heavy brogan type suitable chiefly for hard outside labor. Similarly, the fabric offered for sale was of the coarser type of cloth that, when sewn into garments, would last for more than one season. Few ready-made items of clothing were sold.[14]

The Gibbs store also carried quite an extensive selection of both farm implements and household utensils, the kind of things that could not be made easily by the average farmer. Plows of several varieties, hand tools, horse collars, chains, ropes, axes, etc. for the farm work, plus pots, pans, cups, skillets, knives, forks, and spoons for the home, all figured prominently in the sales column from month to month. In addition, the store carried a rather impressive array of chemicals that were sold to doctors to use in treating the sick. Oils of camphor and cloves, as well as compounds of calcium, potassium, and other elements, all made their way into the primitive remedies that were used to treat the full range of physical maladies. Company records after 1850 do not list the individual items purchased; things are shown simply as "merchandise," so it is impossible to know the amount of patent medicines that might have been sold when they became so popular after the Civil War. One may assume, however, that these magic elixirs and mysterious powders enjoyed popularity in Walker County just as they did throughout the South and that the Gibbs store had them readily available for those patrons seeking physical relief and rejuvenation.[15]

Specific illustrations of the types of merchandise sold and the prices charged can best be seen by looking at some of the credit accounts for the early years of store operations. One of the earliest customers, F. B. Pankey, made the following purchases on September 6, 1841, two days after the store opened:

10 pounds coffee	$2.00
39 pounds salt	$2.34
2 pounds rice	$ .20
1 pint molasses	$ .12
1/3 pounds white sugar	$1.00
1 plow mold	$2.17
1 spinning wheel	$6.00
1 pound nails	$ .15

Another patron, Jeremiah Lauderdale, bought

5 pounds coffee	$1.00
3 tin cups	$ .38
6 thimbles	$ .37
1 butcher knife	$ .37
1 shaving box	$ .38
1 coffee pot	$ .50
1 palmetto hat	$ .37

The purchases of L. B. Giles indicate that his economic position was somewhat above subsistence level. Among other items, Giles bought one yard of Irish linen for $1.50, one skein of silk thread for $.12, and a spelling book for $.19.[16]

In the annual settling of the credit accounts, Thomas and Sandford Gibbs followed procedures initially adopted by Gibbs and Coffin when the store opened. Typically, at some time during the last two months of the year, as they had time to do it, after the crops in the area had been harvested, the two men would go over each account, figure a total of all items purchased during the year, subtract the amount of any payments made by the customer, and come up with a balance remaining to be paid. The Gibbs brothers charged no interest for the credit balances carried through the year the charges were incurred. Having figured the amount owed them by each of the store patrons, the two owners would do nothing until the next time the individual patron came to town, and this was often as late as early spring of the following year. At that time, the bill would be presented for settlement. If a customer could not pay the bill when it was shown to him, he could sign a promissory note that would become due for payment at some mutually-agreed-upon time, usually at the end of six months or one year. Once the note was signed, the Gibbses charged ten percent interest on the total amount owed.[17]

To achieve settlement of the accounts owed them, Thomas and Sandford Gibbs, once again in the tradition established by Gibbs and Coffin, demonstrated considerable flexibility with their customers. Particularly during the early years, 1841-1860, the owners accepted almost anything of value, including services, in lieu of cash. The account of F. B. Pankey, mentioned previously, was settled by crediting him the cost of room and board for Gibbs and Coffin. Pankey earned a further reduction in his bill by cutting four cords of wood for use in the store. Another customer settled his bill by making a pair of saddle bags for Thomas Gibbs, while a third individual put up a horse rack and horse trough at the store and built a stable and a crib in an adjacent lot to retire his indebtedness. Other patrons cleaned the store, built gates, repaired windows, split rails for fencing, did laundry, polished boots, hauled goods for the store, and performed a variety of other tasks to settle their bills if they could not pay cash upon demand.[18]

The Gibbses rarely had to accept property to secure payment for charges made in the store, a reflection, no doubt, of their unwillingness to extend credit to anyone they believed might have trouble paying cash at a later date. On those few occasions when customers did offer land to settle an account, the storeowners frequently sought to work out some other arrangement whereby the patron could keep the land and the store could get its money some other way. The reluctance to accept land as payment stemmed from the perceptive realization that, unless the property were already income generating, it became a burden to the owner. Money had to be spent paying attorneys to perfect and clear the title, a process that often required resurveying the land. Additionally, taxes had to be paid and diligence exercised to prevent encroachments and other forms of trespassing on the property. More importantly, steps had to be taken to make the land turn a profit. If it were already cleared and fenced, the Gibbses, who were not farmers, had to find someone reliable to work it for them. If it were heavily timbered, as most was in Walker and adjacent counties, it had to be cleared before it could be tilled. Land that was left densely forested was of virtually no use to anyone during most of the nineteenth century. Not until the advent of commercial lumbering in the region in the latter decades of the 1800's did large stands of timber become economically desirable.

The value of timberlands in East Texas during the period before the arrival of the lumber companies appears in an anecdote attributed to John Henry Kirby, one of the preeminent personalities in the Texas lumber industry. In the words of an early twentieth century Texas historian,

> A sewing machine agent passed through the eastern section of Texas during this early period [1870's] and Kirby's father traded a tract of pine timber for a sewing machine. About a year later the agent returned and requested the elder Kirby to take the timber land back and give him a cow instead. He had made many attempts to sell the timber during the interval without success. Subsequently, of course, this tract became very valuable.

Similarly, two of the pioneers of the lumber industry in Newton County, Texas, related that timber acreage in that area as late as the 1880's remained so inexpensive that the two of them acquired a league of "good timberland," well over 4,000 acres, for five hundred dollars.[19]

A typical example of the way the Gibbs brothers handled offers of land from store patrons came in the fall of 1860, when A. G. Dumicer tried to give them some of his land to retire his indebtedness. The storeowners refused the offer and suggested, instead, that Dumicer begin paying only the interest on the amount owed them. They believed him to be an honest individual who would pay the entire debt as soon as his financial position improved. On another occasion, L. B. Hightower offered the two brothers the deed to 120 acres of his land to pay off a debt of $197.28 he owed them. The storeowners accepted the deed and agreed with Hightower that the land was worth $180. They then offered to return the deed to him anytime within the following twelve months if he would pay cash to retire the debt instead.[20]

The hesitation at accepting land as revealed in the two instances just cited should not be taken to mean that the Gibbses lacked all interest in acquiring land. As will be shown, the two brothers managed to amass sizable real estate holdings during their lives, but they bought land with very definite ideas in mind as to how they were going to manage it and profit from it. They wanted land that would be a source of income; they were not interested in buying it simply for the sake of having it.

Store customers also traded goods and commodities produced on their farms to settle their debts. Accounts were paid in cowhides, deer skins, bricks, lumber, eggs, livestock, and other products the store could then sell to others. Corn and cotton were the most frequently used goods exchanged for store credit. For the period for which detailed records are available, 1841-1860, corn was usually accepted at a price of fifty cents per bushel. Cotton, over the same period, averaged seven cents per pound when used as payment for store charges. Several of the individuals who traded cotton to pay their store bills earned an extra one cent per pound by delivering the raw fiber to Houston or Galveston, where it was turned over to the cotton buyers who credited it to the Gibbs store. And frequently, the persons hauling cotton to the coast would load their wagons with Gibbs merchandise and return it to Huntsville, where they would be paid cash or given a specified amount of credit in the store. Gibbs paid one cent per pound for merchandise carried from Houston to Huntsville.[21]

The willingness of the Gibbses to accept items other than cash for merchandise reveals a great deal about the store clientele and the service area surrounding Huntsville. Typically, when customers pay for goods with crops or with the performance and completion of work for the store owner, it indicates a severe shortage of circulating currency, necessitating the establishment of a healthy system of barter that can serve to facilitate commerce. As other researchers have demonstrated, the antebellum South endured chronic shortages of capital. The problem was particularly acute in the remote rural areas, far from the urban centers near the coasts or along the large rivers that drained the interior. The storeowners in these outposts had to be able to advance credit to their customers and to be flexible in the schedules and methods of repayment.[22]

In accepting cotton and other non-perishable items to pay for merchandise, the storeowners functioned as factors, or intermediaries, between the producers, that is, the small farmers who traded regularly in the store, and the large commercial supply houses, generally located in large cities, that sold to the Gibbses. Most of the outside firms that served the Huntsville area had their principal establishments in either Houston or Galveston. The steady and growing commerce that developed between the Gibbs brothers and their suppliers served as a conduit whereby goods from outside the area could be brought in and a permanent commercial marketing network could be established and nourished.

The rugged trails between Huntsville and Houston/Galveston on the coast constituted a vital commercial link for the Gibbs store with the outside world. Professional teamsters, as well as private individuals who hauled under contract, were crucially important in maintaining communication with the large wholesale, commission, and banking houses in the coastal cities. Such contacts enabled the Gibbs brothers to buy merchandise in quantity and at prices much more favorable than could have been obtained had they relied solely on the prices and shipping costs quoted by the many travelling salesmen who called on them in Huntsville. The Gibbses usually kept money on deposit, or a line of credit, with several of the private commission and banking houses in Galveston, especially the T. W. House Company, the Ball, Hutchings Company, and the E. B. Nicholls Company, and remained on good terms with the firms, thus securing a position from which to shop around for the best price on any given item.

In addition, through the years the company expanded its direct commercial dealings with banking houses and wholesale suppliers to include some as far away as New York City. Such arrangements permitted the firm to deal directly with large manufacturers in other parts of the nation and pay cash for all purchases made, thus earning further discounts. In early summer, 1860, for example, the Gibbs brothers contacted the Trowbridge Dwight Company, a clothing manufacturer in New York City, to report that they had just spoken with the salesman for the New York firm and would like to do business. Unfortunately, the prices offered by Trowbridge Dwight were five to eight percent higher than Gibbs could get from other suppliers. If prices could be reduced to more competitive levels, the Gibbs brothers were prepared to place large orders and pay immediately with cash they kept on deposit in New York City banks. The Gibbses assured the Dwight Company that they never compared prices with other firms in Huntsville so there need be no fear that others might ask for similar cost adjustments. With some of their other suppliers in the northeast, the two brothers also asked for price reductions and directed the companies to contact the Reed and Tracey banking house in New York for answers to any questions touching on the solvency and integrity of the Gibbs brothers firm.[23] In addition to the Reed and Tracey bank, the Gibbses kept money, at various times, with the Manhattan County Bank, also in New York, the First National Bank in Houston, and the St. Louis National Bank in St. Louis, Missouri. All of these were interest-bearing accounts, and thus generated an income of their own, apart from the financial advantages that accrued from permitting cash purchases.

The considerable economic strength of the Gibbs store, as demonstrated by its scattered financial holdings, distinguished it markedly from other Southern country mercantiles, most of which, as other researchers have demonstrated, suffered from chronic undercapitalization, as well as mismanagement. Such stores existed generally at the mercy of the large suppliers outside the South who could dictate their costs to the stores and levy additional charges for transactions made on credit. The Gibbses were spared such arbitrary, and costly, treatment and the wisdom so apparent in the decision to place their money on deposit in large banks so that it would earn interest, rather than just leaving it in the company safe in Huntsville, bespeaks, once again, their astute sense of business affairs mentioned earlier. The rapid success of their store was virtually inevitable and can be indicated dramatically by remembering that early in 1847 Sandford St. John Gibbs had paid $500 for a one-half interest in the firm; by mid 1863, a little over sixteen years later, sales volume alone in the store had reached $4,500 per month.[24]

The rapid growth of the Gibbs mercantile and the solid financial foundation upon which it was based placed the Gibbs brothers in a position from which they could survey their surroundings to find other ways to invest their assets and reap the resulting rewards. Beginning in the early 1850's, their attention turned increasingly toward the state penitentiary, an important fixture in the Huntsville economy, but an institution perpetually plagued with both financial and managerial difficulties. The Gibbses established close working relations with prison administrators and officials and, over the course of several years, the relationship grew and proved advantageous to all of the parties concerned. More importantly, the association with the prison revealed the Gibbses' preference for engaging their financial resources in projects that would stimulate long-term development and benefit the entire region as well as the family firm.

The bill that created a state prison in Texas received legislative approval on March 13, 1848. Among its several provisions, the law called for the establishment of a three-member commission to select a site for the new institution. The location chosen should be no larger than 100 acres and should not cost more than five dollars per acre. Also, it should be in a healthy climate and near a navigable body of water to permit easy access and visitation. The commission began its work almost immediately after passage of the law and by August, 1848, had selected the town of Huntsville as the site for the new prison.[25] No research has, as yet, revealed the reason for establishing the prison in Huntsville rather than someplace else, and nothing in the Gibbs records sheds any light on the question. But there can be little doubt that Huntsville residents welcomed the facility, as it was considered one of the more important agencies of state government at the time and virtually guaranteed the survival of the town.

From the very beginning, prison officials discovered that state legislators resented spending money to care for convicted felons. The penitentiary seldom had funds sufficient to meets its daily expenses and frequently was without resources of any kind. At such times, the institution was forced to rely on the generosity of the citizens of Huntsville to care for the inmates confined. The state installed looms for weaving cotton and woolen fabric in the early 1850's, hoping the cloth would find a ready market and could help defray operating costs. But the looms frequently stood idle, whether from breakdowns or lack of raw fiber, so production seldom reached desired levels.[26]

Prison officials encountered further problems trying to sell the finished products of the looms. Most state officers had had little experience in the business world, so lacked both the background qualifications and the network of professional contacts that would have enabled them to market the prison cloth successfully. In addition, private businesses that manufactured cotton and woolen fabric attempted to sabotage the prison competition by spreading stories to the effect that cloth woven in the prison was poorly made, the work done by sullen, ignorant convicts, and that buying prison-made goods took money and jobs away from free workers who, as a result, could not support their families.[27]

For the first decade or so after the establishment of the prison, state officials relied heavily on the largesse of Huntsville merchants and planters for the wherewithal to operate the prison. Huntsville businessmen extended credit to the penitentiary and to the prison employees, who were often paid their salaries irregularly. Farmers in the area sold food to the prison on credit or gave raw cotton and wool to the institution so the looms could be kept going and the inmates employed.[28]

The Gibbs store sold substantial quantities of goods to the prison through the late 1840's and 1850's and, for several years, provided the clothing issued to the incoming prisoners. In 1852, for example, one of the years the Gibbs store had the clothing contract, it cost the state $7.45 per year to outfit each prisoner in the following items of clothing (value in dollars):

1 pair woolen kersey pants	1.25
1 woolen roundabout	1.40
1 pair cottonade pants	1.20
1 pair leather suspenders	.20
1 hickory shirt	.70
1 white wool hat	1.00
1 pair russet brogans	1.20
1 pair wool socks	.50
TOTAL	7.45[29]

Each of these items, it should be noted, was of a coarser and more durable variety of material that would stand up under the rough prison working conditions.

The commerce the Gibbs brothers conducted with the prison proved to be profitable to them through the years. They sold a great variety of goods to the state yet never raised their prices to take advantage of the distressed financial conditions in which the prison officials often found themselves. Records reveal, for example, that a pair of brogans, or a shirt, or hat sold to the state went at the same price as the same items were sold to regular customers. The profits came in the volume of business handled rather than from any selective pricing of individual items.[30]

As their relationship with the penitentiary matured, the Gibbs brothers found other areas in which, by helping the prison officials, they could also help themselves. Recognizing the difficulties prison officers encountered in trying to market the fabric produced in the institution, the Gibbses made their network of business contacts available. Acting as informal agents, the Gibbs brothers sent notices to wholesalers and supply houses informing the recipients that prison-made cloth, of high quality, was available and orders could be placed through the Gibbs store. Typical of such notices was one sent to the I. T. Westmoreland Company of Danville, Illinois. The Illinois firm was told that the Texas prison had begun turning out high-quality woolen goods that were priced to compete with the same type goods produced in the North. Plain woolens sold for 27 1/2 cents per pound and twills cost 30 1/2 cents per pound. Gibbs bought the woolens in twenty-bale lots so as to be able to offer its customers the lower prices that came with bulk purchases. Over time the business flourished and the Gibbs brothers advanced the prison money, sometimes as much as $8000 at a time, to guarantee procurement of the raw fiber so that regular production schedules could be met. Also, the Gibbs store became the point of contact for individuals in the greater Southeast Texas region who wished to obtain prison goods. Orders from merchants in towns surrounding Huntsville and in adjacent counties were placed at the store, where receipt of the order was noted and the customer picked up the merchandise when it was ready.[31]

A contract drawn up between the Gibbs brothers and state prison officials during one of those times of acute financial crisis illustrates the close relationship that developed through the years between the private firm and the public institution. In the agreement, the Financial Agent of the prison acknowledged an existing debt of slightly less than $9,000.00 owed by the state to the Gibbses. Additionally, the state needed immediately $5,000.00 to carry on the operation of the prison. The Gibbses agreed to loan the money and the state agreed to retire all its indebtedness to the Huntsville firm by shipping one hundred and fifty bales of cotton cloth, made in the prison, to the commercial house of P. Willis and Brother in Houston and Ball, Hutchings and Company of Galveston. The firms were instructed to sell the cloth at the most favorable prevailing rate and credit all sales to the accounts of the Gibbs brothers. The shipping and handling of the cloth goods prior to sale were "in all respects to be at the risk of the penitentiary," and the Gibbses would earn ten per cent on the money they advanced until the debt was retired by the cloth sales.[32] No evidence could be found that revealed the total amount of profits that were earned through the years marketing the prison goods. Judging from the size of the loans, however, and the relatively small risk assigned to the Gibbses, the earnings may indeed have been handsome.

The prosperity that flowed to Thomas and Sandford Gibbs because of their careful management of their affairs brought with it a certain elevated status within their town, plus responsibilities to step forward and help lead civic campaigns to improve their community. By virtually every measure of public approbation, the two men fared well. They were respected, enjoyed the friendship of Huntsville's leading citizens, and gave generously to a number of worthy causes. Evidence of the public esteem in which the Gibbs brothers were held can be found, among other sources, in the pages of a diary kept by one of the more prominent medical practitioners in town, Dr. Pleasant W. Kittrell.

Originally from North Carolina, Kittrell had also resided in Alabama before coming to Texas in the early 1850's. In addition to a flourishing medical practice, he engaged in a variety of business ventures, land speculation, farming, etc., and had frequent opportunity to deal with Thomas and Sandford Gibbs. In his written references to them, Kittrell thought very highly of both men. On one occasion, he wrote that he had

> ever found this firm [T&S Gibbs] kind, generous and liberal to me and I hope ever to be able to make this record of them .... I find these gentlemen in all my business transactions with them to be punctiliously scrupulous & correct, and to me at all times accomodating [*sic*] and obliging.

The only complaint Kittrell ever made about the Gibbses centered on some of their personal habits, not their business methods. The doctor found the two men, at times, to be "rather-Quakerish" for his tastes. He failed to explain what he meant by such a reference, but in the absence of any elaboration, one might assume that he thought the Gibbses a bit too pious, or prudish, in some matters. Notwithstanding this minor criticism, however, Kittrell firmly believed the men to be both "strait & honest."[33]

While comments made in Kittrell's journal cannot be interpreted to represent a cross section, or even a broad sampling, of public opinion in Huntsville, they nonetheless are significant. Kittrell himself was an individual of considerable prestige in Walker County and one who possessed an abiding dedication to the genteel abstractions of personal honor and integrity. His journal entries, moreover, reveal him to have been a very candid individual who would not have hesitated to criticize or condemn anyone who he believed did not exemplify the high standards of a Southern gentleman.

Further evidence of the Gibbses' standing in the community may be inferred from an examination of the kinds of people who traded regularly in the store. Although by the early 1850's there were several other grocery stores and mercantiles in Huntsville, the Gibbses continued to do a large volume of business with most of the doctors, lawyers, teachers, ministers, and other professional people in town, and relations with all appear to have been cordial. Huntsville's most famous citizen of the nineteenth century, General Sam Houston, traded regularly in the Gibbs store and thought so highly of Thomas Gibbs that he named him as an executor of his will and charged him with the responsibility of caring for the Houston children in the event that Mrs. Margaret Houston, the General's wife, died before the children reached maturity.[34]

A measure of the character of the Gibbs brothers can also be seen in the ways they used their influence and position to help others and promote progress in their town. On several occasions the Gibbses assisted persons who wished to start their own businesses by writing letters testifying to the merit and industriousness of the individuals. In one case, they wrote a letter of introduction to the McLain and Buckley Company of New York City recommending a young man named T. A. Gary, of Plantersville, Texas, who wanted to open a general store. The Gibbses explained to their New York correspondent that Gary had very little money but was a person of good and honest character and could be trusted to abide by any agreement that could be worked out to enable him to buy goods on credit. In another letter, also to the McLain and Buckley Company, the two brothers strongly urged the New York firm to sell goods on credit to Byrd Eastham, who wanted to open a mercantile in Huntsville. Eastham had clerked in the Gibbs store for two and a half years but wanted to form a partnership with his brother, Jackson, and go into business for himself. The Gibbses gave Eastham a very warm recommendation, which they concluded by saying that they would have no hesitation at selling to him on credit should he so desire it.[35]

In addition to supporting individuals they deemed worthy of such, the two Gibbs brothers also used their influence, resources, and time to promote organizations and institutions they thought would improve the quality of life in Huntsville. They contributed to the work of the local chapter of the Sons of Temperance and served as officers of the group on several occasions. They also helped promote the construction of a courthouse for Walker County, giving the first $50 to get the building fund under way. Their most substantial charitable contributions, however, they reserved for religious and educational institutions in the town.

The First United Methodist Church in Huntsville, which grew from a small post on the Methodist circuit in the 1840's, became an established fixture in the community in 1854 when land was purchased for the church sanctuary. Thomas Gibbs served as one of the five trustees who arranged for the property acquisition. Sandford Gibbs joined his brother as one of the stewards of the church when the first permanent building was dedicated in 1857. The Gibbs brothers could always be counted upon to provide generous financial assistance in church building programs, to help in the acquisition of new equipment for the church, and to support the ministers who served the local Methodist community. From these beginnings, members of the Gibbs family have continued through the years to play prominent roles in furthering Methodism in Walker County.[36]

Thomas and Sandford Gibbs also directed a good deal of their effort and resources to help establish a strong educational system in early Huntsville. Beginning with the Andrew Female Academy, founded in 1852, and Austin College, established in 1849, the Gibbses were regular contributors to school activities and the many campaigns to raise funds to support the growth and expansion of the institutions.[37] This commitment to the encouragement of education persisted through the establishment of the Sam Houston Normal Institute in 1879, which will be discussed later.

The Gibbses' support for charitable causes and community programs reached its zenith during the years 1861-1865, when Huntsville citizens, like others throughout the South, left their homes and families to join battle against the Union forces during the Civil War. Thomas and Sandford Gibbs contributed money and supplies to help outfit military companies from the area and organized campaigns to carry extra rations and clothing to wounded troops outside Texas. In addition, they cooperated closely with the Walker County citizens' committee established to provide food and clothing to the families of Confederate servicemen in Huntsville. And all of this was done in spite of what appears to have been strong reservations about the war.

To businessmen like the Gibbses, having investments and commercial relations with firms and financial institutions in several parts of the country, a civil war pitting one section of the nation against another would have been an anathema. A war would have jeopardized the security of their holdings in the North, would have disrupted the avenues by which they received their supplies, would have threatened the value of their money, and could have brought destruction of their property. All of these, irrespective of any patriotic emotions they might have felt as Southerners, would have been good reasons to oppose the war. Additionally, the Gibbses had no large investment in slaves that had to be protected. In the years before the outbreak of the Civil War, each of the Gibbs brothers owned a few slaves who worked as household domestics. Thomas Gibbs had a sixty-year-old couple, along with a thirty-year-old woman, working for him, while a forty-six-year-old couple attended to the needs of Sandford's family. The two men periodically made use of slave labor to perform menial tasks around the store, but this temporary help belonged to regular customers who loaned their slaves to work off part of their store debts.[38]

When the time came to vote on the issue of secession, one suspects the Gibbs brothers, because of all the reasons just mentioned, faced the issue with considerable foreboding. The prospect of a prolonged sectional struggle cannot have pleased them and yet, had they denounced secession, they would have had to face the anger of a public feverishly caught up in a pro-war spirit. Nothing in the Gibbs records reveals how the two men voted, but another source asserts that Thomas Gibbs disavowed secession and voted for Texas to remain in the Union. In 1930, Charles Taylor Rather, a Huntsville native born in 1855, reminisced about life in Walker County when he was a boy. One of his recollections was of the close friendship that existed between his father, George Washington Rather, and General Sam Houston. As the younger Rather recalled,

> I remember hearing him [George Washington Rather] say that General Houston, Harvey Randolph, Thomas Gibbs, and he voted together against secession, and that none of them was ever loved as much afterward by those who were on the other side.

Rather's account makes no mention of Sandford Gibbs's feelings regarding disunion, so any conclusions in his case would be even more tentative than those that could be drawn about his brother.[39]

Despite the evidence to suggest that the two men were lukewarm, at best, in their enthusiasm for the war, they nonetheless supported the Confederate cause. Both men committed sizable quantities of their resources to help in the war effort. Beginning in late summer, 1861, the Gibbs brothers bought thousands of dollars worth of Confederate bonds and regularly provided $100 to $500 gifts to help supply individual military units from the area. They also gave to individual soldiers quantities of food, tobacco, clothing, or the fabric from which garments could be made, and Bibles. Typical of the ledger entries showing contributions to the troops one finds the following (value in dollars):

tobacco to soldiers	3.75 value
20 pounds bacon	4.00 value
1 keg molasses	2.50 value
1 bag rye	.50 value
2 Bibles	1.90 value

For the period August 22, 1861, through December 30, 1862, the gifts included, among other things, butter, tin plates, cloth for a flag, a saddle, four pounds of iron, gunpowder, and the cost of making coats for the men. In addition, the Gibbs brothers gave $100 each to Captains Singletary, Rountree, and Branch, the money to serve as a "company fund" for each of the separate units. They gave Rountree an additional $1,000 when his unit found itself in particularly dire straits. No doubt some of the money loaned to others was repaid after the war, but the records indicate that a substantial sum, especially that invested in Confederate bonds, was lost.[40]

Along with their resources, Thomas and Sandford Gibbs gave their time in support of the war effort. In September, 1862, Sandford Gibbs joined the Confederate Army, serving in the command of Brigadier General Thomas W. Blake, brother-in-law to Thomas Gibbs. Sandford's duties focused principally around the procurement of staple food commodities and vehicles in the Texas, Arkansas, and Louisiana areas.[41] Thomas Gibbs, although he did not serve with the troops, helped organize the Walker County Central Committee, a voluntary organization whose membership donated funds to assist in the relief of the families of troops in the Huntsville area. A similar committee was set up in New Waverly. The committee membership contributed a certain amount of money regularly, usually once or twice a year. The leadership of the committee then decided which families needed assistance, and in what form, and made provision for the help to be given.[42]

The Civil War ended in May 1865, and the defeated South, which had suffered enormous economic losses and extensive loss of lives, began the slow road to recovery. Texas had experienced relatively little fighting on its own soil, so was spared the horrific physical destruction that had been visited upon the older Southern states to the east. In the years immediately after the end of the war, however, Texans had to contend with a state economy perpetually poised on the brink of complete collapse. The two Gibbs brothers turned their attention back to their business as soon as the war ended and attempted to salvage what they could of their pre-war financial position. They called upon their former business associates in the North, specifically the Joseph Whitney Company of Boston, to intercede in their behalf with President Andrew Johnson and secure a pardon under the terms of the Presidential Proclamation of May 29, 1865. According to one Huntsvillian, M. C. Rogers, the Gibbses had "suffered greatly" as a result of the war, which they had not supported with any enthusiasm, and wished to have their record of "disloyalty" expunged as soon as possible.[43]

Few contemporary records remain to give a picture of the two men, or of their activities, during the few years following 1865. Those that are available indicate that they rebounded quickly from the problems associated with the war and continued to play important roles in the community life of their town. One description we have of them, and of the greater East Texas area, during this period comes from a visitor who arrived in Huntsville in June, 1866, seeking employment as a teacher.[44]

Martha Ann Otey, widow of Confederate Colonel A. G. Otey, found herself after the war the sole support of two young children, a daughter, Lillian, and a son, George. Job opportunities around her home in Holmes County, Mississippi, were extremely limited, so in March of 1866 she left her children in the temporary care of her parents and journeyed to Texas looking for a position. She carried with her several letters of introduction from prominent Mississippians, all of whom vouched for her competence, her dedication, and her exemplary character. Travelling by boat down the Mississippi River, she visited Vicksburg briefly before reaching the terminus of the river trip, New Orleans. While in the Crescent City, Otey stayed in the St. James Hotel, where she had the opportunity of meeting briefly with Mrs. Jefferson Davis, also a hotel guest. Otey wrote that she called on the wife of the former Confederate president "to pay in person the courtesy due her from *all true Southerners*!"

> I was admitted without delay, she received me cordially. No one was present save Col. Joe Davis [unidentified] which I liked better than a crowded room of elegant chattering birds of fashionable life. She is a large, splendid looking woman, *very dark*, yet highly accomplished and fluent, is just out of Yankee prison in Georgia, on her way to Montreal for her children.

Otey was quite impressed with the former first lady of the Confederacy and recalled particularly her "quiet, unaffected cordiality of manner and sentiment."[45]

After a few days in New Orleans, Otey departed by ship for Galveston and from there inland to Chapel Hill, Texas. She wrote that she was

> perfectly charmed with the country, and only wish I had a home here, *all fixed* to my mind . . . . I believe this is a far better

country. It is healthy I am told, and such a wealth of room, so different from the broken hills and circumscribed lanes of our section of Mississippi.[46]

Leaving Chapel Hill after a couple of days, she went next to Brenham in Washington County. Of the surrounding countryside she wrote:

> We crossed a beautiful prairie in which you could see for 25 miles. Only the real prospect can give you any idea of the beauty of this country. Miles and miles onward stretches the vast sea of living verdure, enamelled with a thousand flowers of every shade, and covered with cattle grazing at leisure. This section is termed the 'blackland,' . . . very fertile. The monotony is varied by skirts of forest, and clumps of trees, ravines containing water and pools.[47]

From Brenham Otey journeyed to Huntsville, where she arrived at six o'clock on a Saturday evening. The driver of the hack in which she had made the trip cautioned her not to stay in either of the hotels in town as they were unsuitable for genteel patrons. Heeding the advice, she spent her first night in the Steamboat House as the guest of the family of Dr. Rufus T. Heflin, president of the Andrew Female College.[48]

After a restful night Otey visited with the Heflin family and prepared herself to meet other personages of the town.

> In the afternoon Mr. Thomas Gibbs, 'the millionaire of the burg,' called on me. He brought his carriage, and insisted on my making his house my home. So, I consented. He and Dr. H both 'armed' me down the front steps as I made my exit from the house in which Gen'l. Houston breathed his last, and rolled off with him to be again kindly greeted by his wife, a very agreeable, kindly lady.[49]

In the Thomas Gibbs home Otey soon met other members of the Gibbs family.

> After tea, Mr. Sanford [sic] Gibbs, his brother, to whom I had

a letter of introduction . . . called with his wife to see me. The next morning he sent me a fragrant bouquet of cape jasmines, with kind inquiries after my health.[50]

She described the Thomas Gibbs home as "very pretty, though not a fine house, yet elegantly furnished."

The appointments of my room are complete, an addition for my special benefit is an elegant stand with a large, finely bound Bible. And for the first time since the surrender, a colored girl stands around to do my bidding, to help me dressing. It brings back the old feeling, to have one's skirts put on, and the folds adjusted.[51]

Describing her short stay with the Gibbses, Otey reported "such kindness I cannot describe. My every want was anticipated . . . ."[52]

The town of Huntsville impressed the visitor with its beauty, especially the tall pine trees, the first she had seen in any quantity since leaving her home. Huntsville, she wrote, was "thriving" and "improving," with five churches, "all well attended . . . ." In addition, the town boasted of "two fine Colleges, the male—Austin College, [the] female—Andrew College."

The Penitentiary is the *most* important building in point of size, and I may add, interest, for they make money there [i.e. it is profitable.] Wagons are constantly coming and going, and the Officers are a *working corps*.[53]

The uncertainties and anxieties Otey felt in searching for employment among strangers were eased completely when, at the conclusion of her short visit, the trustees and administrators of Andrew Female College offered her the position of vice-principal of the school. She accepted the offer immediately and subsequently brought other members of her family to Huntsville where, over the years, they became valued members of the community. Regrettably, Mrs. Otey died of yellow fever a little over a year after moving to Texas.[54]

The courtesies extended to the Mississippi visitor constitute a revealing glimpse into the personalities of the Gibbs brothers. Despite the turbulence and unrest that followed the end of the Civil War, and the personal suffering they had endured, they refused to become sullen and embittered. In the immediate postwar years, theirs were the voices of reason, sanity, and common sense at a time in which extremist political partisanship and economic collapse threatened their state and region. By this time Sandford Gibbs had begun to appear as the more visible of the two, with Thomas leading a more subdued and less public life. The explanation for the role reversal might lie in the lingering hostility toward Thomas Gibbs by those Huntsville citizens who were unwilling to forget, or forgive, his opposition to secession. Another factor may have been illness. Thomas may have begun to suffer the debilitating effects of tuberculosis, the likely cause of his death in the early 1870's. Whatever the case, Sandford assumed the mantle of family leadership and continued to exert a stabilizing presence in his town.

The intense political passions that had played so large a part in the South's decision to go to war in 1861, coupled with the hatred and resentment that had followed the peace in 1865, gave rise to a number of incidents in which intransigent Southerners challenged the verdict of the battlefield by resisting the authority of the civilian and military officials who governed the region. Frequently, the resistance took the form of outrages against black Southerners by those persons who would not accept the new social order that called for racial equality. In some instances, the altercations became quite violent, involving firearms and resulting in the wounding and killing of individuals.

One of the more egregious examples of the factional violence in Texas took place in Huntsville during a session of the district court in January, 1871. The incident began when an elderly freedman, identified as Sam Jenkins, appeared before a Walker County grand jury to report that he had been attacked severely by a group of local citizens. A few days later, Jenkins was found beaten to death near Huntsville. L. H. McNelly, a captain of the State Police, along with a small force of officers, investigated the matter and arrested four men: Nat Outlaw, John McParrish, Fred Parks, and Jo Wright. The four were then taken before District Judge J. R. Burnett for a hearing. W. H. Thorne, Radical Republican and district attorney for the area, reported that after three days of testimony and deliberation, Burnett freed one of the men, Fred Parks, and ordered the remaining three held in the Walker County jail until the next regular session of the district court. Throughout the three days of the hearing, according to Thorne, a number of threats had been made against the judge and the prosecutors by unruly and boisterous friends of the defendants, who boasted that the three accused would never serve time in jail.[55]

As McNelly and his fellow officers attempted to carry out the judge's orders, the defendants pulled out pistols they had concealed in their clothing and began shooting. In the exchange of gunfire McNelly and one other officer were shot. Two of the defendants made their escape out of the courthouse where, according to Thorne, they

> were met by their confederates who armed with shotguns were in such force as to prevent any further attempt to arrest them. Mounted upon horses, shooting off their pistols and yelling like savages, the prisoners followed by their friends made their escape from town.[56]

Based largely on Thorne's description of events in Huntsville, Republican Governor Edmund J. Davis ordered troops into Walker County, declared martial law in the area, and decreed that the citizens of the county would be levied extra taxes to pay for the additional force. The courthouse incident and the ensuing turbulence of the martial law period tried the patience and nerves of everyone in Huntsville, and open hostility to the authorities appeared frequently. And yet, through it all, a few persons distinguished themselves by their ability to remain calm and rational. District Attorney Thorne, who demonstrated little empathy for the citizens of Huntsville in the affair, nonetheless singled out six men for their determination to resist pressures to join the mob. The men had kept their emotions under control and, in the process, had helped stabilize the situation. In Thorne's words, the six "did not in any way give them [the defendants and their supporters] aid or comfort." The six heroes, in Thorne's eyes, included Judge J. H. Benton, Colonel L. A. Abercrombie, Dr. Rawlings, Mr. Bush of Rawlings and Company, County Commissioner Kelly, and Sandford Gibbs.[57]

The declaration of martial law by Governor Davis sparked a prolonged debate over whether such action was justified. Some argued that Davis had acted precipitately and that the situation in Walker County did not require such Draconian measures; others, like Thorne, contended that Davis had acted appropriately to restore order and respect for legal authority. The merits of the action eventually became lost in the escalating political debate between Davis and the Republicans on one side and the Democrats on the other. The fact that the matter, once it became a political issue, could never be resolved to everyone's satisfaction does not diminish, however, the role of those few who kept their composure throughout the unfortunate episode. Indeed, the judicious and reasoned conduct of the six men who stood firm against mob action would appear to constitute the only honorable legacy of the entire matter.

The distinction which attached to Sandford Gibbs as a result of his actions during the period of martial law brought him further attention from state leaders, as well as requests for additional public service. In late spring, 1871, Governor Davis appointed him to serve as one of the directors of the state penitentiary. Joining Gibbs on the three-member board were Peter Royal, a successful builder [building contractor] and leader of the Masonic Lodge in Huntsville, and Strother Green, a prominent leader of the Huntsville black community, who later served as a trustee of the Bishop Ward Normal and Collegiate Institute, a co-educational college for blacks established in Huntsville in 1883.[58] It may be inferred from the appointments to the prison board that all three men held political philosophies closely akin to those of the Republican governor.

During the period in which Gibbs *et al* supervised the administration of the prison, the institution labored through some of its most difficult years. Suffering perpetual financial shortages, prison administrators had to house and provide for a rapidly growing prison population and find some kind of constructive employment to keep the inmates busy. Overcrowding, lack of funding, and public unwillingness to support new taxes ultimately induced the state legislature to lease the entire prison facility, including all inmates, to private businessmen, who agreed to pay the state a specified sum annually for the rent of the institution and the labor of the prisoners. The prison directors had little control over the way in which the lessees worked the inmates but did visit the prison regularly with a view toward making recommendations to improve the management of the facility. On the subject of the mission, or purpose, of the prison, the three directors attempted to inject their thoughts into the protracted, and often acrimonious, public debate on the matter:

> The prison is a penal institution, and is intended as a reformative one, but not primarily, as some people think. In its management, every opportunity should be given for reform and improvement which is consistent with good prison discipline, but not carried so far as to lead the prisoners to believe that they are the injured persons instead of being the transgressors.[59]

The directors came out in favor of certain innovative policies designed to improve discipline and reward good conduct. They lent their support for the enactment of a commutation law that would reduce a prisoner's sentence "by a diminution of time for good behavior." The effects of such a law, they contended, would "counteract the tendency to feelings of despondency, recklessness and revenge." A further inducement to improved conduct and morale would be legislation to provide financial rewards for those inmates who comported themselves according to the rules and who demonstrated good work habits. The directors had in mind paying the prisoners a small amount, $2.00 per month, as long as the inmates performed their tasks satisfactorily. The money would be turned over to the prisoners upon completion of their terms of confinement, or it could be paid monthly to the inmates' families, if such were the choice. The ideas put forth by the directors, along with their call for the construction of additional prison facilities, went far toward raising the level of debate on penal matters amongst the public at large, as well as the elected officials of the state. The careful thought and deliberation that Messrs. Green, Royal, and Gibbs had focused on their prison tasks became apparent when, through the late nineteenth and early twentieth centuries, each of their suggestions won legislative approval.

Even though Sandford Gibbs enjoyed a very cordial association with the prison through the late nineteenth century, he never drew on his relationship to make extensive use of prison inmates to work any of his land. For a brief period in the early 1880's, prison reports identify a joint venture by the name of "Gibbs and Foster" (no identification beyond surnames) as having acquired the services of seven prison inmates, probably to work as farm laborers. Such use of prisoners was common among the large landowners in the area, with the Thomason, Johnson, Williams, and Eastham families employing large numbers of men for many years.[60]

During the same time that Gibbs aided in the formulation of more progressive prison policies, he also lent his support to the campaign to bring railroad service to Huntsville. Late in 1870, the Houston and Great Northern Railroad, a precursor to the International and Great Northern, began construction of a line to run from Houston northward to a point on the Red River, and from there on to the border with Canada. As was the custom, citizens of the towns along the proposed route were invited to offer a cash bonus to the railroad for bringing rail service to their communities. Huntsville failed to come up with the required gratuity, so the rail line bypassed the town. The townsfolk later had a tap line built from Huntsville to connect with the I&GN, thus obtaining rail service, but the failure to attract the main line temporarily stalled development of the town.[61]

The Gibbs brothers stood firmly among those who supported bringing the main line of the I&GN through Huntsville. As the owners of one of the more prosperous businesses in town, they could see the enormous opportunities for commercial growth that the railroad represented. As early as March, 1871, just after the railroad company announced its building plans, the Gibbs brothers began organizing a collection to provide a $50,000 bonus to attract the line to Huntsville. The firm of T&S Gibbs started the collection with a contribution of $9,000, significantly more than any other donation. Other large contributors included Messrs. "Alston and Oliphint," who gave $3,600 and Dr. J. A. Thomason, who contributed $2,700. The Gibbses later supported the construction of the tap line with financial contributions and with a gift of 13.5 acres for the railroad right of way. The tap was completed in March, 1872.[62]

The pleasure and sense of satisfaction that Sandford Gibbs

must have felt at the beginning of regular rail service to Huntsville was short-lived. In mid-May, he received word that his brother, Thomas, had died while visiting in Hot Springs, Arkansas. Thomas's health had been deteriorating for several years, probably as a result of tuberculosis, and he had gone to the Arkansas spa seeking a cure or at least temporary relief from the ravages of the disease. Thomas was survived by his wife Mary and six children. The will he had had drawn up in December, 1870, named his wife and his brother Sandford to serve as executors of his estate.[63]

Thomas Gibbs left all his property and other assets to his wife and six children, with each receiving an equal share. In the inventory and appraisal of Thomas's holdings, the executors had the difficult task of determining his share of property, most of which he owned jointly with others. The contents of the Gibbs store, described as consisting of "dry goods, groceries, hardware, boots and shoes, clothing, medicines, hats, books and stationery, crockery, saddlery, guns, jewelry, store furniture and all other merchandise," were valued at $10,869.87. Thomas's one-half share came to $5,434.94. The store books showed $54,233.88 owed to T&S Gibbs for merchandise charged. Thomas's one-half interest totalled $27,116.94. The books also listed $2,058.22 in debts owed by T&S Gibbs to suppliers and others. One half of this debt, or $1,029.11, belonged to Thomas. The inventory further revealed a total of $81,512.08 in outstanding loans made by T&S Gibbs. Thomas's share of these came to $40,756.04. A tabulation of the cash in the store showed $29,138.07 in gold and $121.80 in paper currency. Thomas's share of these two totalled $14,629.94. Additional assets included the furniture in his home appraised at $857.75, several carriages and buggies valued at $300, plus a one-half interest, with Sandford, in a sewing machine valued at $40.[64]

Other assets included $20,000 in U. S. Government bonds held in a New York City bank, $338.57 in Walker County warrants, $1,427.50 in county jury certificates, $1,087.52 in penitentiary guard claims, and $658.00 in various sheriff claims. The county warrants and certificates, as well as the claims by the guards and sheriffs, consisted essentially of IOU's, or promises to pay, presented by the county or the state in lieu of cash. The sheriff's claims, for example, were usually for costs incurred in transporting prisoners to the penitentiary. The state appropriated a certain amount of money each year to cover such costs, but if the appropriation ran out before the next session of the legislature, there was no money to pay the claim, so an IOU was given. The same situation prevailed at the county level with regard to juror payments and so forth. Often, the persons receiving the payment certificates would need money immediately, so would sell the certificate to someone, like Thomas Gibbs, who could pay cash at the time. The buyer of the certificate generally would discount the amount by five to ten per cent to cover the cost of having to present it later to the county or state to get reimbursement. And frequently the government entity that had given the warrant would refuse to pay it, or would pay only a percentage of the total. In such cases, the persons who bought the warrant from the original owner absorbed the loss.[65]

In addition to the cash and property associated with the store and his home, Thomas Gibbs left substantial holdings in land. Some he owned individually; other acreage he bought with Sandford; and still other amounts he owned with other persons. The listing that follows demonstrates the diversity of his holdings.

1. Lands owned individually by Thomas Gibbs—

Number of Acres	Appraised Value ($)	County
170	170.00	Walker
213	213.00	San Jacinto

Plus seven lots in the city of Huntsville valued at $5,800.00.

2. Lands owned equally by Thomas Gibbs and his brother, Dr. Jasper Gibbs—

Number of Acres	Appraised Value ($)	County
1,280	640.00	Walker
177	90.00	Walker
661	331.00	Walker
320	160.00	Walker
177	90.00	Walker
320	160.00	Grimes
320	160.00	Grimes

638	638.00	Grimes
320	320.00	Grimes
640	640.00	Montgomery
840	840.00	Montgomery
320	320.00	Montgomery
3,127	1,550.00	Montgomery
640	500.00	Leon
1,476	1,476.00	Bexar
73	738.00	Bexar

3. Lands owned equally by Thomas and Sandford Gibbs —

Number of Acres	Appraised Value ($)	County
789	3,903.52	Walker
100	250.00	Walker
511	511.00	Walker
50	50.00	Walker
186	100.00	Walker
500	100.00	Walker
117	201.00	Walker
1,039	1,821.00	Walker
32	27.00	Walker
30	60.00	Walker
200	200.00	Walker
50	100.00	Walker
1,027	789.00	Walker
517 (Farm)	4,000.00	Walker
154	77.00	Walker
1,068	1,602.00	Walker
177	177.00	Montgomery
994	883.00	Trinity
1,200 (Farm)	1,200.00	Liberty
1,304 (Farm)	4,000.00	Ft. Bend

Plus, an unspecified number of town lots in Huntsville, aggregating 80 acres, valued at $8,155.75.

4. Lands owned by Thomas and Sandford Gibbs and J. M. Smither—

Number of Acres	Appraised Value ($)	County
55	55.00	Walker
320	300.00	Walker
214	61.00	Walker

Plus, three lots in Huntsville valued at $916.00.

5. Lands owned by Thomas and Sandford Gibbs and T. W. Markham—

Number of Acres	Appraised Value ($)	County
250	250.00	San Jacinto

6. Lands owned by Thomas and Sandford Gibbs, T. W. Markham and W. T. Robinson—

Number of Acres	Appraised Value ($)	County
601	Not Shown	San Jacinto
414	Not Shown	San Jacinto
285	Not Shown	Walker
200	Not Shown	Walker
154	Not Shown	Walker
738	Not Shown	Walker
160	Not Shown	Walker

The executors noted that Thomas Gibbs also owned several city lots in Minden, Louisiana. These were not listed and appraised, however, as the executors did not know how many lots were involved or their value. Adding all the land, cash, and other property that could be measured, the executors informed the court that Thomas Gibbs's total worth at the time of his death stood at $114,170.37.[66]

Following Thomas's death, his widow Mary returned to live her remaining years in Plantersville, Texas, where she had been raised. All of the children of Thomas and Mary, except Minerva Ann, ultimately moved away from Huntsville as well. Thomas Arthur, who had inherited his father's one-half interest in the Gibbs store, sold his share to Sandford for $2,875.00 in gold. He then moved to San Angelo, Texas, and opened a bank. Through the years Sandford also purchased some of the other children's interests in the lands that he and Thomas had owned together.[67]

When Sandford Gibbs took over sole ownership of the business, he changed the name from T&S Gibbs to S. Gibbs Company and expanded his activities to include investments as well as the mercantile. In every other regard, however, the firm continued to function as it had since its founding. Apart from his business activities, Gibbs continued to find time to help with those public and civic causes in which his influence could be useful. During the late 1870's, he assisted the state in terminating the first lease of the prison and also threw considerable support to the campaign to establish a state normal institute in Huntsville.

When the state entered into its first prison lease, in 1871, the legislature required that upon termination of the lease agreement a full inventory be made of all state property and equipment. The state would then pay the lessees for any permanent improvements made to prison facilities or for any equipment purchased during the lease period. In the event the state and the lessees could not agree on the value of any improvements, a third party acceptable to both sides would be called in to assess fair value. By early 1876, the prison lessees, doing business as the Ward, Dewey Company, found themselves unable to continue in their contract with the state. The company, which had been awarded its lease during the time the Republicans had controlled state government, had lost political favor with the newly elected Democratic administration in Austin and had suffered serious financial reverses that had forced it to default on its labor payments to the state treasurer. Moreover, the lessees had permitted abuse and neglect of prison inmates to reach publicly unacceptable levels. In response to the growing problems presented by the lessees and the rumblings of public discontent with the lease, the legislature abrogated the arrangement with Ward, Dewey and Company in August of 1876 and called for a financial settlement to be made with the Galveston firm. Disagreements developed quickly as the leasing company sought to exact from the state as much as possible, while the state agents just as zealously labored to protect the public interest. Ultimately, an independent arbiter had to be called in to mediate and resolve the many disputes, and the state turned to Sandford Gibbs for assistance. Gibbs's experience through the years working with the prison, plus the cordial relations he enjoyed with the lessees, made him a near perfect choice for the job. According to one Huntsville source, Gibbs acted "with fairness and impartiality on the questions submitted to him," and by early 1877, an appraisal agreement satisfactory to all parties had been completed. The state resumed possession of the penitentiary in early April, 1877.[68]

Within a few years of the successful resolution of the disputes between the state and the prison lessees, Sandford Gibbs performed what, in retrospect, may have been his most important and enduring service for his hometown. The establishment of the Sam Houston Normal Institute in 1879 and its continued prominence as a teacher training institution reflected great credit upon all those Huntsville civic leaders who manifested such a commitment to the growth and expansion of public education. Sandford Gibbs, like his brother Thomas before him, had continued the Gibbs family support for the two colleges in Huntsville, the Presbyterian Austin College and the Methodist Andrew Female College. Sandford served as one of the trustees of the latter and assisted both schools with donations at critical financial junctures in their history. When Austin College left Huntsville in 1876 and moved to Sherman, Gibbs joined with other public-spirited persons to seek a replacement.[69]

The movement to upgrade the quality of training for public school teachers, especially those who labored in the remote rural areas, had its beginnings in New England in the early 1840's as an attempt to develop a type of standardized, or "normal," teacher preparation curriculum. The normal school idea spread throughout the nation, but its arrival in the South was delayed by the disruptions associated with the Civil War. By the early 1870's, somewhat later than in the rest of the nation, politicians and educators throughout the former Confederacy had begun to make up for time lost and embrace the concept of the normal school.

In Texas, the farsighted activities of Dr. Rufus Burleson, president of Waco University (Baylor), in securing financial assurances from the George Peabody philanthropic fund to help establish a normal in Texas spurred state leaders to act. The Sixteenth Legislature, meeting in January, 1879, received a message from the Peabody trustees to the effect that if the state would appropriate $6,000 per year to support a normal school, the fund would match the appropriation and would continue the assistance "from year to year" as long as the arrangement suited both parties. Governor O.M. Roberts endorsed the Peabody suggestion and supported bills in both the house and senate to create a state normal institution. With the legislative process in motion, elected officials from Huntsville began promoting their town as the site for the new school. Citizens of Huntsville offered to donate the old Austin College building, as well as land adjacent to it, to house the institute. The efforts bore fruit when, on April 21, 1879, Roberts signed the bill establishing the Sam Houston Normal Institute in Huntsville.[70]

Having secured the new school for their town, Huntsville leaders had then to retire an indebtedness of a little over $346.00 on the Austin College building, all that remained of the original price of $1,000 for which the Presbyterian Church had sold the structure when Austin College moved to Sherman. Sandford Gibbs had already paid $150.00 of the original purchase price and subsequently paid an additional $50.00 of the remaining debt, bringing his total contribution to $200.00, or one-fifth of the original price. Other substantial donations came from D. D. Alston, $25.00; John Henry, $25.00; B. Eastham, $25.00; A. T. McKinney, $25.00; and Dr. J. A. Thomason, $20.00. Most of these same men, along with other Huntsville residents, further pledged themselves as securities on a $50,000 bond to the state to guarantee the title to all the property belonging to the institute and to insure that the buildings would be put in an acceptable condition for the beginning of classes.[71]

Sam Houston Normal Institute accepted its first students and began operations in the fall of 1879. Sandford Gibbs was then in his 60th year and in apparent good health. His exertions in behalf of the school formed the initial link of an association between the college and the Gibbs family that has endured through the life of the institution. It also came near the end of the first half-century of the arrival of the Gibbs family in Walker County. During the years since the founding of the store, the brothers Thomas and Sandford Gibbs had prospered and had bound themselves irrevocably to the future of the town of Huntsville. The area had been good to them; they, in turn had been good for Huntsville. The two men had shown themselves to be progressive businessmen, with an eye ever focused on the future. Their actions in support of public and charitable causes reveal them to have possessed a deep commitment to the belief that persons of means also had responsibilities to use their position to work for the betterment and elevation of their surroundings. Their efforts to do so improved as well the quality of their own lives. Sandford Gibbs lived out the remainder of his life in Huntsville, where he divided his time and energies between his many business affairs and serving as the head of a large family that included his own children, plus several nieces and nephews. His death came quietly, at his home, on September 30, 1886.[72]

—II—

The Matriarchy of Sallie Gibbs, 1886-1917

The death of Sandford St. John Gibbs in 1886 brought to a close that period in the history of Gibbs Brothers that might be termed "the founding days." Along with his brother Thomas, he had endured the trials and uncertainties that accompany the establishment of any successful enterprise. Moreover, the two had done so during times of great turbulence and political unrest, first with the coming of statehood and later with the Civil War. They had persevered through all adversities and had planted the Gibbs family roots deep in Walker County. The two men left a legacy of public service and business acumen that could serve as a worthy model to all of their descendants. The task that lay before the remaining Gibbses in Huntsville was to continue the family traditions and maintain the farsighted business policies already begun.

Sandford was survived by his wife, Sallie, and seven children ranging in age from eight to nineteen years. His will, signed four days before his death, made ample allowance for each of his survivors provided that certain conditions were met. Sallie was named executrix of the estate, with complete control of all property and assets so long as she remained a widow. In this provision, Sandford exhibited great confidence in his wife's competence and judgement, a strong indication that during his later years he had acquainted her, at least to some degree, with his myriad, and scattered, business dealings. In the process, he had developed a high degree of trust in her ability to carry on in his stead. Specifically, Sallie was given "full power to sell, exchange, invest, and reinvest" any of the property or other assets left to her and to distribute to the children their portions of the estate "according to her own judgement and discretion . . . ." Were Sallie to remarry, however, she would receive a child's portion of Sandford's estate, while the remainder would be administered by Wilbourn Smith Gibbs, oldest child of Sandford and Sallie. Sandford further requested that his "mercantile and other business interests" should continue to be operated as they had been "so long as in the opinion of my said wife . . . it may be to the best interests of my estate to do so . . . ."[1]

The assets left to Sallie and her children consisted of cash, various bonds and warrants, real estate, store merchandise and store accounts, plus personal property. The following list reveals the value (in dollars) of each of the different parts of the estate:

1. Cash on hand and in banks (Deposits in Ball, Hutchings & Co. Bank, Galveston; St. Louis National Bank, St. Louis, Mo.; First National Bank, Houston; and Manhattan County Bank, New York City.)	31,383.14
2. Notes, bonds, and warrants	89,027.74
3. Personal property	6,052.33
4. Book accounts	34,967.83
5. Merchandise on hand	16,718.64
6. Fifty-four bales of cotton	2,060.00
7. One hundred twenty-six head of cattle	945.00
8. Thirty-nine head of horses and mules	1,560.00
9. Fifty-six oxen	933.00
TOTAL THESE ITEMS	183,648.01

The large number of farm work animals—that is, horses, oxen, and mules—in Sandford's estate would appear to offer evidence that he engaged a good many tenant farmers to work some of his lands and made the animals available to those farmers who had none of their own. Gibbs's real property holdings centered on lands, rural and city, in Walker County, although there were large amounts in adjacent counties as well.

Location	Number of Acres	Value ($)
Walker County	19,313.7 (rural)	43,374.00
Willis	Four city lots	750.00
New Waverly	Two city lots	1,000.00
Huntsville	All, or part of 52 city lots, all located on, or adjacent to, the public square	36,600.00
TOTAL WALKER COUNTY		81,724.00
San Jacinto County	4,287.5 rural	5,687.00
Houston County	280 rural	840.00
Brazos County	686.5 rural	345.00
Liberty County	1,280 rural	1,280.00
Henderson County	2,955.5 rural	1,475.00
Montgomery County	160 rural	160.00
Montgomery County	one store lot	100.00
Milam County	150 rural	150.00

The lands above were owned solely by Sandford Gibbs. In addition to these, he exercised partial ownership in other property. The list that follows represents the acreage owned jointly by Gibbs and L.A. Abercrombie, prominent Huntsville attorney and local politician. Each of the two men held a one-half interest in the lands.

Location	Number of Acres	Value ($)
Walker County	2,576 rural	3,035.00
San Jacinto County	449.4 rural	451.00
Trinity County	300 rural	600.00
Navarro County	833.6 rural	3,332.00

The financial value of Sandford's one-half interest came to $3,709.00. The worth of all lands in which Sandford Gibbs exercised some ownership totalled $98,979.00. Adding the land values to the other assets recounted previously brings the total value of Sandford's estate to $282,627.01.[2]

Once in charge of the business, Sallie Gibbs proved herself fully worthy of the trust her husband had reposed in her. Through the years she expanded the business and increased the property holdings left to her and, in the process, provided a comfortable life style for her family. At her death, she left her children a large estate from which they could fashion a prosperous future for themselves.

Sallie E. Gibbs, *née* Sarah Elizabeth Smith, was born October 18, 1844, in Anson County, North Carolina. Her father, Thomas Jefferson Smith, was a wealthy planter and a descendant of English immigrants who had arrived and settled initially in Virginia in 1735. At the age of four years, Sallie began her formal schooling and by the age of fifteen had enrolled in the Greensboro College for Young Ladies in her home state. In that same year, 1859, her family decided to leave North Carolina and move westward to Texas to join kinsmen who had earlier moved to a plantation near Waco. Family elders deemed it preferable for Sallie to remain with relatives in North Carolina to complete her education, but the prospect of such an exciting trip so enlivened her that she prevailed on her parents to permit her to go along. She secured permission by promising to return to school as soon as she had seen the new family home in Texas.[3]

The overland trip from North Carolina to Texas took six months over very primitive, and frequently uncharted, roads. Owing to its financial resources, however, the family was spared the privation and hardship one would have expected on such an arduous journey. As she related later to her children, the men of the family travelled on horseback, while the women rode in two "Rock-a-way" carriages that were "swung high to avoid roots, stumps and ruts in the unimproved roads." The carriages were described as enclosed coaches with two seats facing each other and six windows curtained with "brocade silk." A high seat on the front of the carriage was reserved for the driver. A set of steps inside the coach could be lowered when the passengers wished to descend from the vehicle. A large number of slaves journeyed with the Smith family to take care of household chores. In the words of one family member, "the Smith family travelled in luxury."

> They had a tent for the family and a carpet to spread on the ground. Each night fresh boughs were cut and laid to form springs for the mattress covered by a featherbed. Then the covers of home woven blankets, home pieced quilts, home woven linen sheets and pillow cases over goose feather pillows, made quite a comfortable bed for the weary travellers by the time the family reached the camp site. Slaves built fires and prepared a meal for the entire retinue. Wild game supplemented the supply of food.[4]

Upon arriving in Texas, Thomas Jefferson Smith found the soil and climate around Waco not particularly to his liking, preferring instead the sandy loams of Montgomery County. Accordingly, he purchased sizable amounts of land not far from Plantersville and began to build a large agricultural estate similar to the one he had left in North Carolina.

A month after the family's arrival in Texas, Sallie left Galveston by boat for the return trip to North Carolina. She re-enrolled in school and graduated valedictorian of her class in 1863. The continued fighting of the Civil War, however, prevented her returning home upon completion of her studies. Instead, she remained in North Carolina through the latter months of the war and returned to Texas with her older brother, James, who mustered out of the Confederate Army shortly after Lee's surrender.[5]

Very late in her stay in North Carolina, Sallie and other Smith family women demonstrated a bit of inspired ingenuity in saving family heirlooms from theft by wandering soldiers bent on taking advantage of the chaos and dislocation that accompanied the collapse of government and society in the defeated South. Hearing that a group of undisciplined troops was approaching the family plantation, the women buried all the silver out in the yard and scrambled to find some way to conceal personal jewelry and other precious items. They decided to put the jewelry between the mattresses of one of the beds and have one of the women get into bed and pretend to be suffering from a highly-contagious disease. When the soldiers, in the course of searching the house, reached the bedroom where the jewelry was hidden the Smith women warned them of the sick woman in bed and, after a brief look into the room, the intruders fled the house.[6]

Shortly after her return to Texas in 1865, Sallie met Sandford St. John Gibbs of Huntsville. The meeting, as it turned out, was not an accidental expression of fate or chance. It was very carefully arranged by Thomas Gibbs and his second wife, Mary Blake Gibbs, sister of Brigadier General Thomas W. Blake, under whom Sandford had served during the war and who had married Sallie's only sister, Molly. Sandford Gibbs at that time was widowed, his first wife, Mary, having died in 1863. The courtship between Sandford and Sallie lasted some six months, and on January 30, 1866, the two were married at Sallie's parents' home near Plantersville. The marriage ceremony took place at 6:00 a.m. so that the wedding couple could leave immediately on the ten-hour carriage trip to Huntsville, where a round of parties and celebrations had been planned for that evening.[7]

Although twenty-five years separated Sandford and Sallie in age, all evidence indicates that the union was a strong one that united not only two individuals, but two prominent families as well. Sallie's dowry, which measured in the "thousands of dollars," enabled the two newlyweds to expand upon Sandford's already substantial position and make the Gibbs family one of the wealthiest in Walker County.[8]

For the first twelve years of her married life, Sallie stayed busy bearing and rearing children. Her first child, Wilbourn Smith Gibbs, arrived on November 12, 1866. There followed Mary Alla Gibbs on August 11, 1868; Thomas Clifton Gibbs on February 7, 1870; Sarah Sandford Gibbs on September 16, 1873; and James Philip Gibbs on April 3, 1875. The youngest child, Luteola Gibbs, was born on June 10, 1878. Household maids and governesses were hired to assist Sallie in her child-care duties, but all indications suggest that she spent considerable time with her children and, in the process, exerted a profound effect on their development. The Gibbs offspring received persistent maternal pressure to excel in their schoolwork. At the same time, careful attention was focused on their spiritual growth. The Gibbses counted themselves among the more active members of the First Methodist Church in Huntsville, located across the street from the Gibbs store. Sallie remained a devout Methodist all of her life and required that her children adhere strictly to church teaching. In the view of one of her granddaughters, Sallie's unrelenting devotion to the precepts of nineteenth-century Methodism, and her insistence that her family do likewise, could, at times, make it almost uncomfortable to be around her.[9]

Even if one may assume that Sallie Gibbs possessed some familiarity with the financial dealings and business methods of her late husband, the scope of the task facing her after his death remained formidable. The size of Sandford's estate left Sallie and her family in excellent financial condition; just as surely, however, she had to contend with the enormous burden of keeping the estate together and, if possible, increasing the size and value of the Gibbs holdings. Her two older sons, Wilbourn Smith and Thomas Clifton, aged nineteen and sixteen years respectively at the time of Sandford's death, could offer only limited assistance to Sallie as she struggled to manage the business and the vast land holdings. The two sons could help by running errands and carrying out other chores, but the more difficult decisions, those that concerned planning for the future and guarding against loss, were hers alone to make.

An additional burden arose from the social dictates of the time that severely restricted the activities of women outside the home. A proper woman of the late-nineteenth century confined herself primarily to bearing and raising her children and keeping her house clean and tidy. She supervised her children's education, both secular and spiritual, and limited her activities to those associated with her church or her children's school. Popular opinion held it to be both degrading and indecent for women to enter the masculine world of business. Any woman who did so, according to prevailing wisdom, ran the grave risk of becoming hardened by the world and of losing those genteel feminine characteristics that formed her principal appeal and charm. And, of course, any woman who recklessly flouted societal customs could expect, with all certainty, that her reputation would become sullied and tarnished and would result in a sharp drop in her status within the community.[10]

Sallie maneuvered herself carefully in her predicament. She decided ultimately to keep the reins of power firmly in her hands, as one suspects Sandford would have wished, and used intermediaries as surrogates to run the public parts of the business. Increasingly, as her sons matured, they became her most reliable and important representatives to deal with other businessmen.

For one in Sallie's delicate position, supervising operations in the Gibbs store would have been the most easily accomplished of her several responsibilities. For a good many years, Thomas and Sandford Gibbs had employed clerks in the store to deal directly with customers and take care of the receiving and shipping of large merchandise orders. Sallie, no doubt, continued to rely on store employees to function as they had when her husband was alive. Her two older sons worked in the store as well, maintaining a Gibbs presence in the day-to-day operations of the business. In addition, the two young men could act as Sallie's eyes and ears, reporting back to her regularly and relaying instructions she wished to have conveyed to the store personnel. However, administering the large Gibbs landholdings, spread out as they were over several counties, proved to be a more difficult problem.[11]

In looking after her real estate interests, Sallie had to concern herself with a number of matters that, if not taken care of properly and on time, could have cost her a great deal of money and resulted in irretrievable losses. Lands had to be protected from encroachment by neighboring landowners. Any squatters, or other trespassers, had to be detected and then evicted. Taxes had to be paid or, if deemed excessive, had to be appealed to the appropriate taxing jurisdiction. Diligence had to be exercised also to respond to any threats made against the titles to the land. All of these responsibilities required the presence of someone who could visit the properties regularly and act quickly to protect the Gibbs interests.

Shortly after Sandford's death, Sallie hired J. F. Plyler, a long-time citizen of Huntsville, to look after the Gibbs real estate holdings. Plyler's duties included all of the items just mentioned as well as checking regularly on the individuals who lived and farmed on land rented from the Gibbses. Frequently, the farm tenants borrowed money and supplies from the Gibbs store through the year and repaid their debts with the sale of part of the crops at harvest time. It was therefore essential that Plyler visit the farms regularly throughout the growing season to make certain that the land and supplies were being used for the purposes intended. As two economists of the post Civil War South have asserted, in the act of advancing supplies and credits to tenants, landowners, in essence, accepted the promise of a crop as collateral. It therefore became essential that they "personally supervise the tenants throughout the year" to make certain that a crop was being cared for properly. If, for example, any of the tenants were wasting the supplies advanced to them by the Gibbses, or were damaging the land in some way by their farming techniques, or were not farming the amount of land agreed upon, the Gibbses stood to lose any investment they had made in the farming operation. Over the years, some of the tenants grew to resent the thoroughness of Plyler's inspection-visits and commonly referred to him as "the Prowler."[12]

In the act of hiring Plyler, Sallie took the first steps toward bringing a formal structure to the management and administration of her varied possessions. For a good many years before his death, Sandford had exercised direct control over all parts of his business enterprise, with no apparent need to examine carefully either the amount of work necessary to control each part or the many factors that went into making informed decisions to promote his many and varied financial interests. From her restricted position, however, Sallie lacked such freedom of movement and action. Circumstances forced her to give careful thought to the kinds of information she needed from others before she could make the right decisions. In parceling out responsibilities to those, like Plyler, who acted in her behalf, she initiated the process of dividing company operations into separate management areas so that special attention and direction could be given to each. J. F. Plyler, who worked for Sallie Gibbs for nearly thirty years, became, in effect, the head of what eventually would become the land department of the Gibbs business. Over the years, Plyler and his successors in the position expanded substantially the operations and activities of the land department. Moreover, by devoting essentially all of their attention to land matters, they provided a much more thorough and professional administration of the properties than could have been obtained had they had to spend any of their time dealing with problems in other areas of the company.

Having arranged matters in the land department to suit her needs, Sallie next turned her attention to bringing a greater degree of professionalism to bear on the financial aspects of her business. In this effort, she relied heavily on her two older sons for assistance. The culmination of their labors came in January, 1890, with the establishment of the Gibbs National Bank.

Thomas and Sandford Gibbs had acted as bankers and performed limited banking functions from the earliest days of their business. They had one of the few safes in town where currency and valuables could be protected and, more importantly, they were men who could be trusted to honor their responsibilities to others and to keep accurate records of all transactions so that there would be no questions later as to how money, or other valuables, left with them were disbursed. In assuming the role of bankers, as well as merchants, the Gibbs brothers took their place among the ranks of other general store owners around the state who provided much needed capital to meet local demands.

Throughout the latter half of the nineteenth century, Texas suffered chronic shortages of investment monies that, at times, became acute. The situation was particularly desperate in the interior parts of the state, far from the larger cities, and especially so in the predominantly agricultural sections where small farmers needed loans to enable them to buy supplies until they could harvest their crops. The few banks that did exist, all located in the larger cities, lacked the financial resources to respond to all of the inquiries from all parts of the state requesting loans and assistance. In 1848, for example, eighteen citizens of Huntsville wrote to the president of the Commercial and Agricultural Bank at Galveston requesting that a branch of the bank be opened in their town. They argued their need for a financial institution on the grounds that they were located within a "highly agricultural region . . ." where a bank would be of great service to local citizens. When the banks proved themselves unable to meet the growing need for funds in the more rural parts of the state, local storeowners, and others having some measure of capital at their disposal, stepped into the breach and made limited amounts of money available.[13]

In the opinion of one scholar of the Southern economy, the banking and credit extension activities of Southern storeowners constituted their "greatest contribution" to the well-being of local agriculture. By advancing credit, in either goods or funds, to local farmers, the storeowners ensured that the cultivation, planting, growth, and harvesting of the crops could proceed according to seasonal dictates. Local farmers frequently turned over a portion of their harvested crops directly to the storeowner to retire any indebtedness. They, along with others, might then sell the remainder of their crop to the same storeowner, who, having collected a substantial quantity of local agricultural products, would then make provision for shipping the material to markets outside the area. In the process of serving as a buyer and shipper of local crops, the storeowners laid the foundation for an expanded agricultural marketing system that would link local farms to distant markets. The availability of at least limited amounts of credit and capital was essential to the operation of such a system.[14]

The obvious need for credit and capital, however, did not guarantee that a particular merchant/banker capable of providing assistance would succeed and prosper. As a recent researcher has noted, in the absence of strong banking regulations at either the local, state, or federal level, those merchant/bankers who succeeded over the long term were those who had earned the trust of the local people. And in deciding with whom they would trust their financial future, people usually turned to those persons with the broadest business experience, along with an established reputation for honesty and integrity.[15] By any of those measures, the Gibbses fared well and, not surprisingly, residents of Huntsville very early on turned to them for banking services.

The early daybooks and company ledgers of the Gibbs store from 1841 through the Civil War years reveal considerable financial activity of the type one generally associates with a bank. In one case, the Gibbs brothers advanced $8.85 to Mrs. Lucinda Parker of Bedias so that she could pay her taxes. No interest was charged on the money. They also collected no interest on a loan of twenty-five cents to John McAlister made in January, 1846. As a general practice, the Gibbses levied no interest charges if the loans were small, as in the two instances just cited, or if the money was paid out in small amounts through the year as part of a customer's regular commerce with the store. For example, one individual, R. C. Burne, amassed a bill of $149.69 for the year 1845. Most of the indebtedness came from merchandise purchases, but $51.00 of it resulted from cash advances. Thirty-five dollars was given to Burne directly, while $16.00 was paid by the Gibbses to other individuals at Burne's instruction. At the end of the year Burne took care of his debt by turning over to the Gibbs brothers a quantity of cotton sufficient to cover the amount owed. No interest was figured into the account.[16]

Through the late 1840's, the 1850's, and the early 1860's, the Gibbs banking operation expanded steadily with most transactions involving small loans to regular store customers to provide short-term financial help. Also, since the store was centrally located on the public square where everyone would visit when they came to town, persons living in the rural parts of the county frequently would leave funds with the Gibbses with instructions to pay out the money to other persons the next time the latter came into the store. An individual, for example, who might have lived in a remote part of the county and seldom travelled to town would leave money at the Gibbs store to be paid to another person who lived in another part of the county. Such an arrangement relieved the former of the necessity of travelling a great distance to pay his debt. When the Gibbses paid the money, as per instructions left with them, they carefully recorded the transaction in the ledger books so that all parties would have a record of the deal and be protected against any further claims. A typical example of the financial transactions the Gibbses handled for other parties occurred in early January, 1863, when the two brothers accepted $200 in Confederate money from an individual named Edwin Jardine. The money was to be given to another person, Stephen Newton, on or about March 1, 1863, if Newton complied fully with the provisions of a contract that had been drawn up between the two men. The contract was left with the Gibbses, with authorization to determine whether Newton met the requirements of the agreement and to pay out the money if he did. In another case, J. J. Carruthers of Victoria County left $400 cash at the Gibbs store to be paid out to H. G. Smith, a Walker County resident, the next time Smith came to town. The Gibbses charged Carruthers $10 for handling the transaction. The journal of Dr. Pleasant W. Kittrell also lists several occasions when he relied on the Gibbs brothers to handle his payments to persons whom the doctor had not been able to meet on his periodic trips to Huntsville.[17]

By September, 1879, the volume of banking business conducted by Sandford Gibbs had reached the point that he found it necessary to establish a separate banking department in the Gibbs store. A month later he hired a youthful G. A. Wynne to manage the banking section as well as keep books for the mercantile. Even though the creation of the Gibbs private bank came at a time when all banking was still in its infancy in Texas, there is evidence to indicate that there had been an earlier banking house established in Walker County. According to Joe E. Ericson, a chronicler of early Texas bankers, the firm of Smith and Wynne opened a bank in Huntsville sometime during the year 1873. Little information remains concerning this bank so that questions about the identity of the owners, the nature of bank operations, or even the length of time the bank remained in business cannot be answered. Thomas C. Oliphint, who lived in Huntsville during the last half of the nineteenth century, has recalled that a firm known as "Smith and Wynne" operated the first "cotton wharf," that is, a cotton buying business, in Huntsville and that the Wynne in the partnership was Magruder Wynne, father of G. A. Wynne. Expanding a bit on Oliphint's recollections, it is reasonable to assume that Smith and Wynne conducted some simple banking functions, such as loans and advances to cotton farmers, as part of their cotton purchasing business, and the younger G.A. Wynne managed to learn enough of the banking business from his father to make himself valuable later to Sandford Gibbs. Wynne remained in the Gibbs banking department after the death of Sandford Gibbs and played an important role in helping the Gibbs family expand its banking operation.[18]

One of the reasons that private banks such as the one operated by the Gibbs family grew to be such a vital part of the rural economy in Texas, apart from the chronic need for capital, lay in the reluctance of most Texans to permit the growth of a large and well-established system of state-chartered banking institutions. Walter Buenger and Joseph Pratt, in their study of the development of the Texas Commerce Bank in Houston, have shown that most citizens of nineteenth-century Texas, true to their Jacksonian roots, harbored an abiding mistrust of large banks that might "transfer their significant economic power into political power." Public suspicion of banks and bankers manifested itself in the several state constitutions approved in 1845, 1861, and 1876, all of which placed a ban on state-chartered banks.

"To most Texans, banks were a big business which could rob the common man of his democratic rights and impoverish the unwise investor or depositor."[19]

In the absence of any well-ordered system of state-regulated banks, private financial houses inevitably appeared and operated according to whatever policies they chose to establish and implement. As a result, there was considerable disparity in the stability and strength of the individual institutions. Those lacking sound management, or without adequate capital reserves, went under and took all of their depositors with them. Over the course of time, as the number of private bank failures increased, there was further fastened on the public mind the negative image of bankers as thieves.[20]

In something of a paradox, however, by the late 1880's, the antipathy toward private banks began to give rise to an increased interest in national banks as a safer alternative for one's hard-earned money. National banks had to meet federal government requirements as to the amount of capital needed to begin, and sustain, bank operations. In addition, periodic inspections by federal bank examiners, designed to promote the development of sound banking practices, conferred an extra measure of protection for depositors that could not be had with the private banks. In the fall of 1889, according to G. A. Wynne, "there was considerable agitation over the question of a national bank for Huntsville." In a meeting with Sallie Gibbs and her eldest son, Wilbourn Smith Gibbs, Wynne recommended that the family respond to the public interest by requesting approval to establish a national bank. The proposal, in Wynne's words, "was readily agreed to," and the group mailed the application to the Comptroller of the Currency for a charter to set up the First National Bank of Huntsville. While awaiting federal government approval, B. A. Shepard, president and principal stockholder of the First National Bank in Houston, suggested to Wynne that the bank be named to honor Sandford Gibbs. Wynne presented the idea to Sallie, who was "pleased" at the suggestion, so the name of the new institution was changed to read the Gibbs National Bank.[21]

Organized officially on January 14, 1890, the Gibbs National Bank began operations with a "paid up capital" of $50,000. The five hundred shares of stock, each valued at $100, were held by the following individuals (values in dollars):

1. Mrs. Sallie Gibbs	266 shares	26,600.00
2. Wilbourn Smith Gibbs	100 shares	10,000.00
3. W. W. Adickes	50 shares	5,000.00
4. L. A. Abercrombie	30 shares	3,000.00
5. J. W. Thomason	20 shares	2,000.00
6. G. A. Wynne	20 shares	2,000.00
7. T. H. Ball	10 shares	1,000.00
8. R. S. Rather	3 shares	300.00
9. F. B. Robinson	1 share	100.00
TOTAL	500 shares	$50,000.00

The shareholders selected six of their number to serve as the first board of directors of the new bank. L. A. Abercrombie, W. W. Adickes, T. H. Ball, W. S. Gibbs, Mrs. Sallie Gibbs, and G. A. Wynne constituted the board membership. At their first meeting, board members selected W.S. Gibbs to serve as president, along with W. W. Adickes filling the position of vice-president, and G. A. Wynne as cashier. J. F. Estill was hired as the bank's bookkeeper. The board decided that the bank would be open for business between the hours of 8:30 a.m. and 4:30 p.m. every day of the week, except Sundays and state-observed holidays. In its final actions at the first meeting, the board set up a committee of three of its members to conduct quarterly audits of bank operations and authorized the cashier to spend up to $1,500 for the necessary bank furniture and fixtures, to include a substantial safe with a time lock.[22]

Sallie's election to the board of directors of the Gibbs National Bank does not appear to have been merely a gesture of courtesy toward her. She had committed a considerable sum of money to the venture, and her frequent presence at board meetings was essential to protect her investment. Neither was she the first woman in Texas to serve as a bank director, although she was very likely the first who actively performed the duties associated with the position. Marilyn McAdams Sibley, in her biography of George W. Brackenridge, has written that Eleanor Stribling and Eleanor Brackenridge both began serving on the board of the San Antonio National Bank in the 1870's, thus pre-dating Sallie's service by over a decade. Sibley goes on to note, however, that the San Antonio women took no active part in the management of bank affairs. They "did little except fill places and refrain from interfering."[23]

The minutes books of the Gibbs bank board of directors reveal that Sallie served on the board until her death and occasionally attended board meetings. Regrettably, the books provide little information beyond mentioning the items discussed and the decisions made, so it is impossible to know the degree to which she might have participated. It bears pointing out, however, that her influence on bank policy did not depend necessarily on her presence at all of the board meetings. Indeed, it would not have been necessary for her to be present at any. Her son, W. S., could have kept her well informed of board activities and could have relayed to other board members any suggestions, recommendations or observations she desired to make. From a memorial to her shortly after her death in 1918, one gets the clear impression that indeed she had a good deal to say about how the bank operated, regardless of whether she attended board meetings. The bank directors, in their remembrance of her, credited her with having provided the kind of "counsel and advice" that had "contributed greatly to the success" of the bank. While admittedly, the language of such tributes often tends toward hyperbole and excessive adulation, the fact that direct and specific reference was made to her value as a source of advice may, indeed, point to significant contributions she made to the evolution of bank policy through the years. One thing is certain: her effective control of over two-thirds of the bank stock would have guaranteed that her voice would have carried considerable influence on those occasions when she chose to use it.[24]

The offices of the Gibbs National Bank, rented from Sallie for $400 per month, were housed on the ground floor of the brick building located on the northeast corner of the intersection of 11th Street and Sam Houston Avenue (directly north of the northwest corner of the courthouse square). Thomas and Sandford Gibbs had built the brick structure in 1860 to replace the wooden building they had purchased from Pleasant Gray in 1842. At the time it was completed, both men boasted that the new building was much more comfortable than the older quarters and, of equal importance, was fireproof. To make room for the bank, the Gibbs store was moved to the ground floor of the building immediately east of the new brick building. The offices of Sallie Gibbs's varied enterprises were located above the bank. Above the Gibbs store, living accommodations were provided for the unmarried clerks who worked in both the bank and the store. The windows of the living quarters were covered with heavy iron shutters that, when closed, could prevent unlawful entry into the premises. Presumably, the closed shutters would also serve to deter any after-hours departures by Gibbs employees seeking amusement and excitement in Huntsville's night life.[25]

The bank, particularly, could be very strict in forcing its employees to comport themselves according to accepted local customs and standards. In the case of one bank employee, W. F. Smither, the board of directors, undoubtedly because of admiration for the young man and for his abilities, went out of its way to rescue him from his own excesses. Smither had gone to work for the bank as a bookkeeper in 1901 at a salary of $480 per year. He performed his work satisfactorily, causing no complaint, but in his personal life he was reckless and profligate with his money. In 1903, Smither requested a salary increase to $60 per month. The bank directors agreed to the raise but told Smither he would be allowed to receive only $50 per month of the higher pay. The remainder would go into an escrow account that he could collect at the end of the year if he "quit spending his money extravagantly and . . . saved enough out of the $50 per month to pay all of his debts . . . ." The board's confidence in Smither was well placed. Within a few years he had his finances under control and in 1906 saw his salary boosted to $75 per month.[26]

Although Gibbs family members had majority control of the new national bank, none of the assets or liabilities of the defunct Gibbs private bank were transferred to the new financial institution. In the words of G. A. Wynne, the Gibbs National Bank "started at the bare boards on the ground floor and built up." Deposits on the first day of business totalled $6,283.35; loans approved came to $30.00 and a profit of $1.00 was earned. From these beginnings bank assets grew steadily. At the end of its first year of business, total deposits had climbed to $91,394.18. Net earnings for the same period came to $5,667.10, from which the directors voted a dividend of $4,000, that is, eight percent of the total capital stock of $50,000. With the exception of the year 1921, following two years of cotton crop failures, the bank paid dividends of at least eight percent every year through 1922, the last year the Gibbs family exercised majority control. The largest dividend, two hundred percent, was paid in 1910 from excess earnings that had accumulated through the years since the bank's opening. Average dividend payments over the thirty-three year period 1890-1922 totalled twenty-five percent, or $12,500 annually. Each $100 share earned a total of $815 over the same period.[27]

Throughout its existence, the Gibbs National Bank served primarily the needs of the small local farmers who borrowed money, usually at eight to ten percent interest, using their crops or their land as collateral. Payment of the loans after the fall harvest enabled the farmers then to borrow for the following year's planting, if they needed additional money. Bank records do not reveal any systematic procedures for collecting overdue loans, and other indications suggest that the bank officers exercised considerable flexibility and often carried the farmers well beyond the loan due dates. On several occasions, for example, federal bank examiners criticized bank officers for having too many loans out and for doing too little to collect them. The examiners customarily demanded that immediate steps be taken to collect the outstanding notes or write them off as losses. Through the period 1890-1922, the Gibbs National Bank lost a total of $31,953.05 from bad or uncollectable loans, an average of almost $1,000 per year.[28]

In part, the reluctance by bank officials to push too strenuously for payment of the overdue loans, particularly those for which land may have been used as collateral, resulted from an apprehension that to press for collection might lead them to have to foreclose on the land. The bank did not relish this prospect. It wanted money in return for the money it loaned. The acquisition of land brought with it the burden of paying taxes on it and of finding someone responsible to work it, problems that became especially onerous if the land were located in the more remote parts of Walker County or in an adjacent county, where inspection was difficult and time consuming. An illustration of the headaches bank officers had to endure with land ownership can be seen in the protracted maneuverings to unload a piece of rural property during the first decade of the twentieth century. Sometime prior to 1904, the bank acquired slightly over 820 acres in Ft. Bend County, just to the southwest of Houston. In

January, 1904, board members, after having tried to sell the land earlier, decided to pay for fencing the property so as to make it more attractive to anyone interested either in farming or pasturing cattle on the land. Fifteen months later, and still without a renter, the board instructed the cashier to go to Ft. Bend County, assess the strengths and weaknesses of the property relative to other lands in the county, and recommend ways the land could be made "revenue producing." When, after all of this, the bank still had no takers, board members instructed the cashier to sell the land for whatever price he deemed best. As of October, 1910, over six years after coming into possession of the land, the bank was still trying to get rid of it.[29] There is no mention in the records that the land was ever sold, thus indicating that it remained part of the bank assets throughout the history of the Gibbs National Bank.

In a retrospective look at the development of the bank during its first twenty years, W. S. Gibbs reported the overriding philosophy of the institution as having been "conservativeness tempered with liberal treatment of worthy patrons and legitimate help to legitimate local enterprises . . . ." The bank, in his view, tried to be a good neighbor and citizen of Huntsville by promoting the healthy economic development of the area. He noted that only once, during the Panic of 1893, had the bank ever had to discount and get rid of any of its paper. At that time, owing to extreme financial exigencies, the bank sold two small notes, aggregating a total of $7,500.00, to its correspondent bank in St. Louis, Missouri. Thus chastened early in the history of their institution, bank officers thereafter kept a careful eye on the amount of loans granted so as to be able to withstand future economic reversals. The rewards for the cautious lending policies came in 1907, when, in the midst of another national financial collapse, the Gibbs National Bank was able to respond to all requests for cash made of it.

> [The] bank not only took care of all its depositors' checks as presented, but went further and supplied all the cash for the monthly payrolls of the two State institutions located in Huntsville, viz: the State Normal School and the State penitentiary, doing so [at a time] when the State Treasurer was unable to supply the cash to meet its [*sic*] current expenses, the various

> State depositories having refused to honor his calls for cash against the State's money deposited with them.[30]

No evidence exists to confirm conclusively any assistance given by Gibbs National to the state institutions in Huntsville during the 1907 depression. On several other occasions, however, the bank advanced lines of credit and provided low-interest, long-term loans to local state officials who sought to keep the state institutions open and functioning normally during times when no money from the state was forthcoming. Given the patterns of continued support for the college and the penitentiary, both of which figured prominently in the economic welfare of Huntsville, it is reasonable to assume that the bank would have stepped in and provided any assistance it could during times of economic hardship, such as those that prevailed in 1907.

In a further response to the Panic of 1907, the bank also temporarily eased its lending policies so as to provide increased assistance for the many farmers struggling to make it through the depression. The additional loans permitted the farmers to hold their cotton until prices improved. Those persons with loans already due for repayment were given extensions until "such time as they saw fit" to sell the cotton and repay their notes.[31]

> It is declared the sense of the board that it is best not to force our customers rather preferring to let them use their own discretion and it is also deemed to advance other farmers, not our customers, on their cotton at the rate of about 8-10 cents per pound for the present. [32]

The decision by the directors to advance credit to their regular customers as well as to those farmers who had not previously done business with Gibbs National reflects, without question, a large measure of concern for the economic welfare of the inhabitants of Walker County. After all, it was not in the bank's best interest to permit large segments of the local population to suffer prolonged financial hardship. Moreover, by advancing credit to persons who had not formerly been served by Gibbs National, bank officials laid the foundation for an expansion of bank business in the future. Many of the new customers probably had never dealt with any bank, so any kindness shown them would likely eventuate in their opening accounts with the Gibbses. But there was another factor that loomed large in the minds of board members and provided additional motivation to reach out and solicit new business. As of 1907, Huntsville had another bank.

In 1905, the state legislature, responding to entreaties from the Texas Bankers Association, authorized the establishment of a state banking system. Capitalization requirements under the state law were less than those mandated for a national bank and, in consequence, the number of smaller banks grew dramatically. By the end of 1907, 346 state-chartered banks functioned in Texas. The Huntsville State Bank, founded in 1907, billed itself as "the bank of the people," in contradistinction to the family-controlled Gibbs National. The new bank sought to represent itself as the institution open to everyone rather than to just an elite few who sought only to further their own special interests. Such an appeal would generate considerable enthusiasm and support in an area like Walker County, steeped in the anti-bank traditions of the rural South. Residents of the area had fervently embraced Populist Party assertions in the 1890's that big-monied interests oppressed small farmers and wage earners. The presence of the Huntsville State Bank dictated that for the remainder of its history, the Gibbs National Bank would have to function in a much more competitive environment than the one that had prevailed in 1890.[33]

During the first decade or so that Sallie Gibbs exercised control of the family assets, she also had to devote large amounts of her time to her duties as a single parent. Although hired domestic help freed her from having to do the more tedious household chores, she bore full responsibility for inculcating in her children healthy, positive attitudes toward study, work, and the obligations of citizenship. By 1900 all of the Gibbs offspring had reached maturity and had begun their respective careers. The kind of life each of them led confirms that Sallie fulfilled her parental duties satisfactorily.

Wilbourn Smith Gibbs, usually addressed simply as "W. S.," was the first to reach a level of age and maturity that enabled him to assist his mother with the family business. In addition to serving as president of the Gibbs National Bank, W. S. devoted much of his energies to negotiating with the several lumber companies that, by the late 1890's, had begun to show considerable interest in the large stands of timber on Gibbs land. The success he enjoyed in the timber business, as well as in his other economic ventures, reversed earlier indications that had portended limited achievements for him.

During his formative years, W. S. had demonstrated only an average ability in his studies. He received his early education in the Huntsville public schools supplemented with private tutoring at home. He did well in math, but found the humanities and social sciences difficult. By 1883, shortly before his seventeenth birthday, he convinced his parents, against their better judgment, to let him drop out of school for a while. In granting permission, however, Sandford and Sallie told him that he would have to work in the fields if he did not attend school. W. S. accepted the challenge and through the 1883-1884 school year labored on one of the Gibbs farms. He produced a respectable crop of cotton that year, but the experience convinced him that his future lay in something other than agricultural stoop labor. In the fall of 1884, he entered Southwestern University, a Methodist school in Georgetown, Texas.

In college, as in his earlier public school career, W. S. showed strength in math but had trouble with the humanities. He persevered through the 1884 and 1885 school years, but dropped out for good following the fall term, 1886, and the death of his father. Upon his return to Huntsville, he moved back in with his mother to help with the younger brothers and sisters and maintained that residence until his marriage in 1900 to Annè Nugent of Jackson, Mississippi. The first two children, both sons, born to W. S. and Annè died at birth. The third child, christened Wilbourn Sandford, was born in 1909 and was the only child of W. S. and Annè's to reach majority age.[34]

The second child of Sandford and Sallie, Mary Alla (known as Star), was the only one of the Gibbs daughters to reside in Huntsville after her marriage. She attended the Huntsville public schools for her early education and did her college work at Kidd-Key College, a Methodist school in Sherman. In 1898, Mary Alla married Henderson Yoakum Robinson, a local businessman and descendant of Henderson Yoakum, the well-known early Texas historian. Mary Alla had two children, both sons: Wilbourn Thomas Robinson, born in 1899, and Herndon Yoakum Robinson, born five years later. During her life, Mary Alla steadfastly supported all activities of the First Methodist Church in Huntsville and, through the years, generously contributed to all church programs.[35]

Thomas Clifton Gibbs, Sallie's third child, was one of only two of the Gibbs children to marry before reaching age thirty. After graduating from high school in Huntsville, Thomas Clifton, like his older brother, W. S., attended Southwestern University, where he "excelled in his studies" but did not graduate. In 1893, shortly after his return to Huntsville to help his older brother run the family business, Thomas Clifton married Jamesetta Hunt, daughter of Judge and Mrs. Thomas M. Hunt of Caldwell, Texas. Thomas and Jamesetta Gibbs had five children, four of whom reached maturity: Pauline, Cecile, Edith, and Anne Kathleen. The first child, named Thomas Clifton Gibbs, Jr., died in infancy.[36]

Sarah Sandford Gibbs, fourth child of Sandford and Sallie, was the only one of the Gibbs children to leave no heirs. Educated like her older sister at Kidd-Key College, Sarah Sandford was thirty-seven-years of age when, in 1910, she married Dr. Oscar Norsworthy, a Houston physician. The Norsworthys had one child, whom they named Oscar, who died a few days after birth. Dr. and Mrs. Norsworthy lived most of their years together in Houston, but late in their lives moved to the drier climate around San Antonio.[37]

James Philip Gibbs, fifth child and youngest son of Sandford and Sallie, was the only one of the Gibbs children to complete post-graduate university work. According to one of his daughters, James Philip exhibited considerable academic potential very early in his life. His mother, recognizing this ability, encouraged the young man, at times quite forcefully, to apply himself to the study of medicine. Accordingly, after preparatory study in Huntsville, James Philip attended Southwestern, where he was awarded his degree in 1896. There followed one year at Stanford University, and in 1901 James Philip received the M.D. degree from the College of Physicians and Surgeons at Columbia University in New York City. After a brief period of specialized study in Europe, Dr. Gibbs opened his medical practice in Houston, concentrating his work in the field of pediatrics. In 1905, while serving as president of the Harris County Medical Association, he married Mary Brent McAshan, daughter of James

Everett McAshan, pioneer Houston banker. Dr. and Mrs. Gibbs had three children, Virginia Sandford, Sarah Elizabeth, and James Philip, Jr.[38]

Luteola Gibbs, Sallie's youngest, followed her two older sisters to Kidd-Key College, but transferred and completed her studies at Randolph-Macon Women's College in Virginia. She married Henry Houston Hawley, a successful Dallas businessman, in 1903 and bore two children: Henry Houston, Jr., and Sarah Alla. Following their marriage, the Hawleys lived the remainder of their lives together in Dallas.[39]

By the time the last of her offspring had married and left home Sallie's older children had begun to present her with grandchildren to bring the joy and bustle of youth to her home in her later years. Virginia Gibbs Smyth, daughter of Dr. and Mrs. J. Philip Gibbs, has described how excited she and the other grandchildren were when they visited their grandmother in Huntsville. Although Sallie could be stern and disapproving of disruptive, or otherwise unacceptable, behavior, she could just as surely show great love and warmth for the children. She had a small room, just off her bedroom in the Gibbs home, where she kept fruit, candy, and other specialties from the store stashed away. When the children were good she would take them into the room, redolent with pleasurable fragrances, and reward them with some of the treats, or perhaps give them a couple of shiny new nickels they could then take downtown and spend on whatever they chose.[40]

Mrs. Smyth also remembered that Sallie was very much the head of the Gibbs clan. All of her children and their spouses deferred to her judgement and sought her advice and recommendations on all major decisions. Moreover, she demanded that she be kept well informed of all business activities. As late as 1905, with Sallie in her sixty-first year and her eldest son approaching forty, she still received regular detailed reports of company activities. In the accounting of that year, W. S., somewhat apologetically, informed his mother that earnings were down from previous years, owing to the cancellation of several uncollectable debts, coupled with a decrease in cotton production. Precise figures were given for each account, along with notations to explain losses and adverse performance. The true significance of the document, however, lies not in the numbers themselves but rather in the comprehensiveness of the report and in the minute rendering of all areas in which the company either earned or lost money. The fact that such an all-encompassing review of company operations was prepared for Sallie at a time in her life when one might have expected that she would have begun to retire and turn matters over to her children clearly points to her central importance in directing the continuing fortunes of the Gibbs properties.[41]

An examination of the 1905 annual report reveals that by that date the Gibbs store had ceased to be the important source of income that it had been for Thomas and Sandford Gibbs. By 1905, the Gibbses earned most of their income from land. Rural acreage, as well as property in Huntsville, generated income through rent, land and timber sales, and from the sale of products produced on the land. Net receipts for 1905 totalled $36,975.12. Of this figure, $19,720.76 came from farm rents and from the sale of cotton and cattle grown and produced on the land. An additional $5,415.76 was generated from the sale of some parcels of land, or from the products, like timber, grown on the land. Rents for town property totalled $5,707.55. The only other major source of income, $10,379.03, came from the interest paid on money loaned by the company. No mention is made of any separate income from the Gibbs store, suggesting that by the early twentieth century it had become little more than a provider of basic supplies and equipment for tenants who farmed Gibbs land. Profits and losses on farm supplies sold in the store would have been figured as income or loss from the farm accounts.[42]

The emergence of land management as the principal source of Gibbs income arose primarily from an increase in the value of the land and what it would produce. Cleared lands, like the natural prairies in Walker and adjacent counties, had always been valuable as farmland; and evidence demonstrates that, at least as early as the late 1860's, a few people had tilled Gibbs land. Customarily, the tenant farmers either paid an annual cash rent or surrendered part of their crop as payment for use of the land. With the arrival of railroads and lumber companies during the latter decades of the nineteenth century, the previously less valuable heavily timbered lands began to offer attractive possibilities for steady profits as well. The Gibbses were quick to take advantage of the new opportunities available in timber sales and saw company profits increase dramatically during the early decades of the twentieth century. The dense stands of pine in eastern Texas constitute the western edge of a belt of timber that begins in the hills and mountains of the Deep South and extends across the Mississippi River through Louisiana and Arkansas, then across the Sabine River into Texas. In the words of two recent historians of the lumber industry in Texas,

> The forest region of East Texas includes all or parts of forty-eight counties and encompasses more than 36,000 square miles . . . . [An] area as large as the state of Indiana and larger than any of twelve other states. It extends from the Gulf coastal plains on the South to the Red River and from the Sabine to an irregular line somewhat short of the 96th meridian, where the pine forests thin out and give way to scattered groves and open prairies.[43]

Making up roughly ten percent of the state's total land area, the forests of East Texas consist of many different types of trees, with several species of pine in overwhelming preponderance. When settlers began to push into eastern Texas in the first half of the nineteenth century, large stands of the towering and majestic longleaf pine, interspersed with other varieties of evergreens as well as hardwoods, could be found in a pocket in extreme Southeast Texas. Through the centuries, the longleaf had thrived and flourished in the area, but theirs was a precarious existence. They did not reproduce as easily and quickly as did their natural competitors, and any outside influence could threaten their continued dominance. Early logging methods, particularly the commonly used clearcutting techniques, tipped the natural balance against the longleaf pine and in favor of other varieties, especially the shortleaf and loblolly. Today, few stands of longleaf pine remain.[44]

The two latter mentioned species, i.e. shortleaf and loblolly, were initially found in a circular swath that surrounded the longleaf. The shortleaf predominated in the northern section, while the loblolly flourished in the southeastern portion of the surrounding band. Loblolly pine, or a mixture of loblolly and assorted hardwoods, has tended through the years to move into the areas formerly occupied by the longleaf.[45]

The exploitation of the East Texas timber for commercial purposes coincides roughly with the arrival of Anglo-Americans in the quarter century before the Civil War. Most early sawmills were small and portable, rather primitive as well, and served a clientele that lived chiefly in the local areas around the mills. A few larger operations that could produce limited amounts of lumber for shipment elsewhere were located along the upper Texas coast, where the rivers and bayous that drained East Texas emptied into the Gulf of Mexico. The saw logs were shipped down the rivers to the mills, and the finished lumber was then loaded aboard ships for transport to other points. The major obstacles to large-scale lumber production during the mid-nineteenth century arose from two sources: an insufficiency of capital and expertise to build and operate large commercial mills, and the lack of any effective means of penetrating the thick forests to remove the logs economically. Not until several years after the Civil War, with the arrival of the railroads and of experienced sawmill entrepreneurs, did lumbering in East Texas become commercially feasible.[46]

The first railroad to push into the East Texas pine forests was the Houston, East and West Texas Railway. Chartered in early spring, 1875, the railroad was built in a north-northeasterly direction out of Houston toward Shreveport, Louisiana. By 1882, construction had reached as far as Angelina county, and the line was completed to Shreveport in 1886. As the track was extended into the forest, lumber mills sprang up along its roadway and the process of cutting timber for shipment out of the area got underway. Shortly after the HE&WT started building out of Houston, the Texas and New Orleans Railroad initiated construction of a line that would run northwesterly from Beaumont to Dallas. The Atchison, Topeka, and Santa Fe also built into East Texas, thus providing a third major line from which a number of shorter roads and connecting tram lines could be built to reach the major timber stands.[47] The arrival of the railroads in the pine forests of East Texas, and the beginnings of commercial lumbering, ended forever the region's deadening isolation from the rest of the world. New towns sprang up along the railroads; new jobs became available in both the sawmills and the logging camps, and all three offered opportunities for enterprising individuals to escape from the grinding existence of the small subsistence-level farms.[48]

Concurrent with the construction of the railroads, experienced lumbermen, many from other parts of the country, heavily-armed with both expertise and financial resources, arrived to begin the exploitation and extraction of the now accessible timber resources. A number of legendary family fortunes grew from the Texas lumber industry, represented by names such as Alexander Gilmer, Joseph Kurth, John Martin Thompson, and Thomas Lewis Latane Temple, among others. Three individuals, however, stand above the rest for having done the most to establish and develop the modern lumbering industry in Texas. Henry Jacob Lutcher and G. Bedell Moore brought state of the art technology to the East Texas woods, while John Henry Kirby built a lumbering empire that, at one time, was the largest in the South and overshadowed all his competitors. During the first half century of commercial lumbering in Texas, from the late 1870's to the 1930's, more than 59 billion board feet of finished lumber were processed from the East Texas pine forests, and these three men played major roles in that bonanza.[49]

The Messrs. Lutcher and Moore, experienced lumbermen from Williamsport, Pennsylvania, journeyed through East Texas during the late winter of 1877 looking for new timberlands. The forests in their section of Pennsylvania were rapidly nearing exhaustion, and the two wanted to locate a new home for their milling operation. They travelled east-northeastward from Houston, examining mill site possibilities near where the Neches and Sabine Rivers emptied into Sabine Lake. They also explored north of Beaumont and Orange, examined the size of the trees, the density of the timber per acre, and by the end of the year had built their first mill, described as "the first truly large, modern sawmill in the state of Texas," in the town of Orange, along the Sabine River. Lutcher and Moore bought thousands of acres of heavily-timbered land throughout Southeast Texas and southern Louisiana (typically paying less than $3.00 per acre) and established a number of timber-related companies, i.e. railroad tram lines, window and door companies, mercantiles, turpentine operations, coastal shipping and freighting firms, and even deep-sea vessels for shipping Lutcher and Moore lumber to trading partners throughout Central and South America and the Caribbean.[50]

A decade or so after Lutcher and Moore established their mill in Orange, a young man practicing law in Woodville began to take an interest in the financial promise of the East Texas forests. Originally from the small settlement of Peach Tree Village, not far from Woodville and also in Tyler County, John Henry Kirby correctly sensed that the efforts of the early lumbermen in Southeast Texas portended a bright future for the timber industry. Sometime in the late 1880's he met several Boston investors, among them Nathaniel and George Silsbee, who were attempting with little apparent success to establish a cattle ranch on some East Texas acreage they had purchased. Kirby convinced the men that a better economic future lay in buying timberland on which nice stands of trees could be sold at a handsome profit to the lumber companies that were beginning to reach into the pine forests. Kirby and his out-of-state investors began buying thousands of acres of densely forested land in Texas and Louisiana and also began constructing railroads and tram lines that would facilitate access to the timber. By the dawn of the twentieth century, the Kirby group had acquired ownership or stumpage rights, i.e. the right to cut and remove trees, on nearly 1,000,000 acres and had sold their railroad lines to the Atchison, Topeka, and Santa Fe Railway, the directors of which agreed to loan money to Kirby for additional timber purchases.[51]

The Spindletop oil discovery near Beaumont in 1901 changed the economic landscape in Texas and provided additional financial and investment opportunities for industrious individuals like Kirby. At a meeting of the American Lumbermen's Association in Chicago in March, 1901, Kirby convinced his investors, and some others, that under all the timberlands they had bought in Southeast Texas there likely could be found large pools of oil, such as had been discovered nearer the coast. It only remained for enterprising persons to go in and begin exploration. Ultimately, Kirby's efforts yielded two new companies, the Houston Oil Company and the Kirby Lumber Company, both established in July, 1901. The two companies would, in effect, be exploiting the same land, but at different levels: one at the surface, the other underground.

> The oil company, capitalized at $30 million, would own and control more than a million acres of East Texas timberlands and would engage in oil exploration and development. The lumber company, capitalized at $10 million, was to own and operate fourteen to sixteen sawmill facilities and related properties.[52]

The Kirby Lumber Company went on to become, by any measure, a major American corporation, and to say that it dominated lumbering in East Texas is to understate the matter by a great deal. At one point, the Company ranked as the largest enterprise of its kind in the South and Kirby became a force of considerable magnitude in the Southern timber industry.

> Displaying tremendous energy and drive, great personal magnetism, a confidence-inspiring presence, a venturesome spirit, and a thorough knowledge of pine timber, Kirby took advantage of a combination of fortunate circumstances to build a great lumber empire . . . . Among the feudal baronies of East Texas during the bonanza era, Kirby held the largest and the most absolute fief.[53]

Although few East Texans could approach Kirby's wealth, power, and prestige, the growth of the Texas lumber industry that he had done so much to facilitate brought a generally higher level of prosperity to all owners of East Texas timber. Landowners, as well as speculators, joined the lumber companies in buying as much as possible of the heavily timbered lands that had previously been worth very little.[54] The Gibbses, with their many years of experience buying and selling East Texas lands, were admirably fixed to take advantage of the new opportunities made possible by the increases in land values. Representatives of the Gibbs family joined the rush and competition, attempting to acquire large tracts in the most desirable areas, that is, with good timber and with easy access. Sallie, working through her sons, bought approximately 108,000 acres during the time she directed the Gibbs business operations, with most of the purchases coming in the first decade of the twentieth century. The largest percentage of these acquisitions came in Walker and adjacent counties, although she also bought good stands of timber in a few counties situated at some distance from Huntsville. The list that follows gives approximate totals of the timber acreage purchased by Sallie during the period 1886-1916, the years she directed the family business:

1. Brazos County	170 acres
2. Grimes County	3,642 acres
3. Henderson County	132 acres
4. Houston County	2,609 acres
5. Jasper County	340 acres
6. Liberty County	2,724 acres
7. Madison County	4,602 acres
8. Montgomery County	600 acres
9. Newton County	12,598 acres
10. San Jacinto County	22,332 acres
11. Trinity County	2,272 acres
12. Walker County	52,000 acres
TOTAL	104,021 acres

Additionally, Sallie acquired close to 4,000 acres in the far West Texas counties of Castro, Hale, and Swisher. These lands appear to have been purchased solely for speculation purposes, as they formed part of the fertile high plains that began to be settled around the turn of the twentieth century. By 1917, the Gibbs lands in West Texas had been sold to settlers or to other speculators and land companies.[55]

Deed records reveal that with the exception of approximately 19,500 acres obtained at sheriffs' sales, Sallie paid the prevailing market price for all of the land she bought. East Texas timberlands during the late nineteenth and early twentieth centuries sold for prices ranging from $1.00 to $10.00 per acre. The value of the land varied according to the types and quantity of trees on it, the accessibility of the land, and the desire of the owner to sell. Of the acreage bought at sheriffs' sales, Sallie paid an average of ninety cents per acre; that is, she paid $17,690.10 for 19,562.3 acres. 442 acres were in Madison County; 2,246.4 were in Grimes County, with the remainder in Walker County. The largest single acquisition from a sheriff's sale came in 1900 and included the acreage in Grimes County just mentioned, plus 11,284 acres in Walker County. The sale came about following the death in March, 1898, of George W. Grant, land speculator and former sheriff of Walker County. At the time of his death, Grant had very little money and had incurred sizable debts against his estate. He owed Sallie Gibbs slightly over $60,000 in loans, plus interest, going back as far as 1891. Confronted with this situation, the Walker County Court appointed two long-time Huntsville residents, E. L. Angier and W. H. Woodall, to conduct an inventory and appraisement of Grant's properties. The court further appointed Thomas F. Sims, mayor of Huntsville, to serve as administrator of the Grant estate. The appraisers determined that Grant left lands in both Walker and Grimes counties that were valued at $25,520.00. To retire the indebtedness against the estate, the court ordered that public notice be given of a sale, "for cash" only, of the Grant lands. The sale was ordered to be held on Tuesday, October 2, 1900, between the hours of 10:00 a.m. and 4:00 p.m. at the courthouse door in Walker County, Texas. On the day of the sale, representatives of Sallie Gibbs tendered the highest and best cash bid, $10,735.00. The court accepted the sale and the land was transferred to the list of Gibbs properties.[56]

It should be borne in mind that the laws governing sheriffs' sales of property in Texas, with the strict legal requirement that the lands be sold for cash only, gave individuals like the Gibbses a distinct advantage. In Huntsville at the turn of the twentieth century few persons had ready access to cash in quantities that would have enabled them to compete against the Gibbses when Sallie decided she wanted to bid for a piece of property. It bears noting also, as an indication of the degree to which Sallie maintained control of her business, that all property acquired was bought in her name and the deeds of title listed her as the owner. This situation prevailed up to the time, in late 1916, that she relinquished control in favor of her older sons, W. S. and Thomas Clifton, who by that time were nearing middle age.

Shortly after she began acquiring timberlands, Sallie entered into a long-term business arrangement with the Palmetto Lumber Company, a firm with headquarters in Houston and mills in several East Texas counties. Under the terms of the agreement, W. S. and Thomas Clifton Gibbs, acting for their mother, bought large quantities of heavily timbered lands in Newton, San Jacinto, and Walker counties. All of the marketable pine on the land they sold to the Palmetto Lumber Company at modest, though profitable, prices. The Gibbses retained possession of the land itself, with all mineral reservations, plus all the hardwood timber. The money expended in purchasing the land and timber was treated as a loan which Palmetto repaid at ten percent interest over several years from the proceeds of the lumber sales.[57] The Gibbses extended further credit to Palmetto anytime the lumber company experienced shortages of cash to meet its operating expenses or needed funding to buy out other sawmills or to upgrade equipment in its existing mills. The close relationship between the Gibbs family and the Palmetto Lumber Company proved to be inordinately beneficial to both parties. The lumber company was able to rely on the financial resources and business skill of the Gibbses to acquire timber on a regular, dependable basis that permitted the company to maintain a steady supply of sawlogs to meet the production schedules of its mills. Moreover, company officials found it much easier to borrow money from the Gibbses than from the usual sources. As a private family-owned company, the Gibbses could be much more flexible if the lumber company could not repay loans precisely when they came due. Commercial banks could not have afforded to be as generous in accepting late payment as were the Gibbses. Palmetto officers deemed the relationship to be so advantageous for them that during the first two decades of the twentieth century, the most prosperous period for the company, they relied almost exclusively on the Gibbses for their timber needs. For its part, the Gibbs family realized handsome profits as well. They made money from timber sales to Palmetto, from the money they loaned the lumber company, and from the very substantial quantities of land that they obtained as a result of years spent buying timber for Palmetto. Over the life of the agreement with the Palmetto Lumber Company, the Gibbs family came into possession of well over 12,000 acres of land in Newton County, over 14,000 acres in San Jacinto County, and an undetermined, but considerable, amount of acreage in the northern parts of Walker County. With most all this acreage, the Gibbses also acquired all, or the largest share, of the mineral rights.[58]

The combination of factors that came together at the turn of the twentieth century to make lumbering both feasible and profitable presented opportunities that had to be grasped quickly before they passed or were seized by others. The decision to commit company resources to investments in timber constitutes one of Sallie's more enduring services for her family. Appropriately, it represented the culmination, as it were, of her stewardship of the Gibbs assets. On October 18, 1916, a little over two weeks beyond the thirtieth anniversary of the death of her husband, Sallie Gibbs celebrated her seventy-second birthday. Her health had been declining for several years and, probably sensing that her time was ending, she had to make some disposition among her children of her enormous property holdings. During her tenure as the matriarch of the Gibbs family, Sallie had more than tripled the amount of land left her by Sandford. Her total holdings, which stood well in excess of 120,000 rural acres and close to one hundred city lots in Huntsville, were substantial enough, if managed properly, to provide a comfortable living for many generations of Gibbses to come.

The enormous burden of responsibility imposed by the potential wealth the land represented and the concern that she act in the best interest of all her children no doubt brought Sallie many anxious moments as she pondered the future after her own death. To have divided the lands equally and fairly among her children would have been virtually impossible to do. The lands were widely scattered and were not all of the same potential or value. Some were heavily timbered, while others had been clearcut and had few marketable trees on them. Some were situated in rich bottomland areas near large rivers, while others were made up of the comparatively poor red dirt soils of the East Texas uplands. Some had all mineral rights, while others did not. Some were located in areas readily accessible from Huntsville, whereas others were situated at some distance from Walker County. And finally, though local taxes on some of the lands were relatively low, others required more costly sums from year to year.

Moreover, even had an equitable division of the property been possible, further complications would have appeared. It could not have been guaranteed that all of the children would have managed their shares wisely and profitably. Those with a keen sense of business would have done well, while the others, with little feel for the worlds of finance and land management, would likely have lost their shares through the years. As to the capabilities of individual grandchildren, great-grandchildren, and succeeding generations to manage their shares of the land carefully, the likelihood that all would continue to enjoy a comfortable livelihood grew even more problematic. Upon consideration of all the problems inherent in a division of her properties, Sallie rejected that option. She chose instead to leave all of the lands to all of her children, who would then jointly administer the holdings.

Among many long-time Walker County residents there exists a belief in the story, probably apochryphal but nonetheless widespread, of how Sallie was able to convince her children of the absolute necessity of keeping the Gibbs lands intact as a solid economic unit. According to the story, at various times during her children's adolescence Sallie would send them out of the house into the yard and tell each of them to bring back a twig, or tree branch, about the thickness of the index finger. When all had returned with their twigs, Sallie would take one of the sticks, hold it firmly at each end in her hands and bend it until it broke. She would then take one of the broken pieces, combine it with the other five sticks, grasp all in both of her hands and demonstrate that the bundle could not be broken as the single twig could. This was done, of course, to illustrate that if her children remained closely committed to each other and kept all of their shares of the land together, they could better withstand the periodic economic reverses they were bound to suffer. They would prosper much longer than if they attempted to act independently of one another.

To repeat: the tale probably constitutes little more than a bit of colorful local exaggeration, but it does represent a simplistic rendering of the philosophy that went into the establishment of the Gibbs firm of today. It also helps explain part of the reason for the continuing success of the company. The details surrounding the formation of the business by the Gibbs children will be discussed in the next chapter. Suffice at this point to say that Sallie's entreaties were accepted and on January 1, 1917, the firm of Gibbs Brothers and Company came into existence. For the remainder of her life Sallie left the burdens of the business to her two older sons. Her health continued to decline and in the early morning hours of May 27, 1918, Sallie Gibbs died.[59]

In looking back at the years during which Sallie directed the various Gibbs business operations, it is virtually impossible to overstate either her importance or her impact on the evolution of the modern Gibbs firm. When she took over the business following her husband's death, she had to master quickly the inner workings of the several parts of the family operation and provide the leadership that would protect her interests and promote an expansion of her holdings. Her six minor children could offer little help to her during her early years of widowhood. As her children matured, she was able to rely on them for assistance, especially the two older sons, but available evidence indicates that, until very late in her life, she kept the reins of control firmly in her hands. The enormous expansion of the Gibbs property holdings under her tutelage and the initial steps she took to bring a formal and more professional administrative structure to her business attest to her skill and determination as a businesswoman. Had her accomplishments been limited solely to these things, she would merit respect and admiration. Her most significant contribution, however, came in the influence she exerted to persuade her children to keep the Gibbs property holdings intact.

Much credit for the establishment of Gibbs Brothers and Company, and for its success through the years, must be attributed to Sallie. Although factual evidence to sustain such a contention is scarce, the few documents that are available point to her as the prime force involved. In none of the extant correspondence of either Thomas or Sandford Gibbs, or of any of the older children of Sandford and Sallie, does one find any discussion, or mention, of the desirability of the children forming a partnership to administer the family lands jointly. Nor does the will of Sandford Gibbs indicate that he envisioned the creation of any type of management arrangement such as was put together by his children. The genesis of the idea to have all the Gibbs children administer the family holdings jointly developed some time during the thirty years that Sallie directed the company. Perhaps the original idea was not hers but was, instead, suggested to her by an acquaintance, or by one of the attorneys the company routinely employed to perfect land titles. The true source likely will never be known. Irrespective of its origins, however, Sallie obviously found the idea attractive and used her considerable influence over her children to see it translated into reality. If any opposition to the formation of a partnership developed, there is no record of it, and any initial reluctance or hesitation on anyone's part would have disappeared quickly once the obvious benefits of such an arrangement were explained. The unanimous endorsement of the partnership agreement, manifested initially by the six children of Sallie and Sandford Gibbs, has continued through the years to elicit strong support from the Gibbs descendants and explains, in large part, the continuing success of the company.

—III—

The Emergence of the Modern Firm, 1917-1940

The formal agreement that established Gibbs Brothers and Company was signed in Huntsville on December 30, 1916. All six children of Sandford and Sallie Gibbs committed their collective resources to the firm "for and during such period of time as shall be mutually agreeable to [all] the said parties."[1] The family had indeed come a long way since Gibbs and Coffin had opened their hardware store a little over seventy-five years earlier. By 1916, the combined efforts of Sandford and Sallie Gibbs had produced an accumulation of real property and other assets that would provide a solid financial foundation for the families of their six children. Indeed, if managed properly, the holdings could maintain future generations of Gibbses in positions of considerable comfort and privilege.

Under the terms of the partnership agreement, the Gibbs children declared the purpose of their firm to be "to engage in the buying, holding and selling of lands, notes, claims and securities of all kinds . . . ." The agreement specifically excluded the Gibbs general mercantile from the remainder of the jointly held property. It would not be included as part of the partnership holdings, thus reinforcing the earlier observation that by the early twentieth century it had ceased to function as a significant source of revenue for the company. Each of the six children would have an equal share in the company and, correspondingly, would share equally in all profits and losses from year to year. The six agreed further to place the "active management" of the firm in the hands of W. S. and T. C. Gibbs, who would be paid "a reasonable salary . . . to be fixed by the other partners" and considered as "part of the expenses of the operation of said partnership . . . ." In a general statement of their duties, the two managing partners were empowered

> to sell any of the assets [of the firm] and to invest the proceed of such sales in such property, or securities, as in their judgement would be for the mutual advantage of the members of said co-partnership, and to re-sell, re-invest and to make purchases, sales and loans, without limit, or restriction, where and whenever in their judgement the interests of said partnership will be promoted thereby . . . .[2]

The managing partners additionally were instructed to prepare an annual accounting of profits and losses within sixty days of the first day of each new year showing earnings for the year. A copy of the report was to be given promptly to each partner, along with "his or her equal share of the profits" from the previous twelve months.[3]

In perhaps its most important provision, the partnership agreement sought to place restrictions on the number of future partners in the firm by vesting ownership solely in the lineal descendants of Sandford and Sallie Gibbs. To accomplish such a limitation, the agreement stipulated that all "undistributed assets of said co-partnership . . . shall continue to be the separate property" of the six Gibbs children and their offspring. The annual earnings of the firm would be distributed to the partners and would constitute community property. Such earnings, however, could not be re-invested in the firm, thereby conferring partial ownership on the spouses. In restricting ownership only to Gibbs descendants, the original partners sought to prevent spouses from holding any assets in the firm that they might, at some point, attempt to have partitioned out of the total partnership holdings. Husbands and wives of Gibbs descendants could enjoy the profits of the partnership and could see their children become partners, but could not exercise any rights of ownership in the firm themselves.[4]

On the same day the partnership agreement was signed, the Gibbs children fell heir to all of the property left them by their father, plus the lands acquired through the years by Sallie. In all, the heirs divided among themselves approximately 140,000 rural acres in the sixteen Texas counties of Brazoria, Brazos, Castro, Grimes, Henderson, Houston, Jasper, Leon, Liberty, Madison, Montgomery, Newton, Polk, San Jacinto, Trinity, and Walker. The largest holdings were found in San Jacinto County, approximately 25,000 acres, and Walker County, where the Gibbses owned slightly over 83,000 rural acres and all or parts of eighty-five city lots in Huntsville—that is, all of forty-three city lots and parts of forty-two more.[5] These lands formed the foundation upon which the future of Gibbs Brothers and Company would be built.

The establishment of a partnership necessitated that serious thought be given to the way in which decisions were to be made in governing the company. Even though the partnership agreement conferred broad discretionary powers on W. S. and T. C. to run the company in the manner they deemed best, it turned out that the most important decisions affecting the firm were made, in effect, by all of the partners. That such an arrangement would develop was not surprising in a company like Gibbs Brothers, in which all the owners were blood relatives, each having an equal stake in company profits as well as an equal responsibility to absorb any losses. The two older brothers would oversee the day-to-day operations of the business, would serve as official representatives of the company, and would maintain all contacts with other firms wishing to conduct business with Gibbs Brothers. All major decisions, however, such as those concerning whether to expand into new business ventures, or those that involved the potential loss of large sums of money, were made only after full consultation with all the partners.

The structure of the office force and the division of responsibilities within the firm changed very little following the formation of the co-partnership. The company's reliance on the rural acreage for the lion's share of its revenues insured that the land department would retain a position of vital importance in the company. J. F. Plyler, the original land man hired by Sallie Gibbs, had left the Gibbs family employment by the time the partnership was formed. His place was taken by J. William Oliphint, an A&M educated engineer, who had gone to work for Sallie in 1908. Oliphint's duties focused almost exclusively on timber production, requiring that he oversee dense stands of trees scattered throughout the Central and Southeast

Texas area. Oliphint spent a good deal of his time in the forests, making certain that all provisions of the contracts to cut Gibbs timber were strictly met and that Gibbs Brothers' interests were protected. He also devoted much of his energies to surveying all of the land as it was acquired to ensure that property lines were marked in accordance with the boundaries as specified in the deeds.[6]

The dictum requiring that all profits be distributed directly to the partners each year obviated the necessity of hiring large numbers of people to manage the liquid assets of the company. Each of the partners assumed personal responsibility for his or her share of the profits. Within a few years of the formation of the partnership, however, some of the family members preferred to let the office staff manage the profits for them. Accordingly, individuals were hired for the purpose of recommending and making investments on behalf of individual family members. This branch of the business, which might be termed the financial section, has functioned through the years much like a private bank for those family members who wish to make use of its services. Additionally, with the passing of time, the financial section has taken over the responsibility of managing the property within the city limits of Huntsville. Personnel in the financial section see to all maintenance, improvements, and remodeling of city property as well as to collecting all rents due. The money required to operate and maintain the Gibbs Brothers offices and to pay employee salaries comes from periodic assessments of each of the partners.[7]

For the first three years of the firm's existence—that is, from 1917 through 1919, when W. S. and T. C. directed the company as managing partners—their younger brother, Dr. J. Philip Gibbs, served with the American military forces. Dr. Gibbs enlisted during World War I, received a commission as captain, and served with military units in Georgia and Kentucky. Late in the war, he was posted overseas as part of the American Expeditionary Force. In 1919, Dr. Gibbs received an honorable discharge from the military, whereupon he returned to Houston and closed out his medical practice. Shortly thereafter, he moved his family to Huntsville and on January 1, 1920, joined his brothers as one of the managing partners in the family firm.[8]

The decision by Dr. Gibbs to forsake his career in medicine and join his brothers in running the family business seems to have arisen from a couple of sources. First, he no doubt wanted to see the firm succeed and felt that his talents and assistance could be of benefit to the family. In addition, however, there is reason to suspect that by 1920 he had lost the desire to continue to practice medicine. One of Dr. Gibbs's daughters, Virginia Gibbs Smyth, remembers that her father never demonstrated any all-consuming dedication to the medical profession. Indeed, it appears he did not really want to become a doctor at all, but did so primarily as a result of Sallie's persistent urging. He nonetheless acquitted himself well in his profession and enjoyed considerable success, but after nineteen years he retired from the medical field and rejoined the Gibbs family in Huntsville.[9]

At the time Dr. Gibbs took up his duties with the family firm, Gibbs Brothers and Company had just completed its third year of partnership operations. Company income for the first thirty-six-month period, while substantial, was by comparison well below the earnings that would come in subsequent decades. Of greater importance, the sources of revenue for the first three years of operation fell into a pattern that portended many years of dependable earnings. Figures in the different income categories would fluctuate from year to year, but as all were tied closely to the land, they could only increase as the value of the real property rose. Since so large a part of the economic growth and business expansion in twentieth century Texas has grown out of mineral extraction and the exploitation of other natural resources, those individuals and corporate entities owning large blocs of land and sizable portions of the mineral reservations have been in a position to enjoy sustained and growing profits from their holdings. Throughout the entire period, 1917 through 1940, Gibbs Brothers earned its greatest income from land sales, from rent payments for use of the land, from the sale of timber, and from monies in the form of lease payments from oil companies seeking the right to explore for petroleum under Gibbs land. Ironically, although the company has profited enormously in recent years from leasing fees, it earned only negligible income from royalty payments prior to 1940. Indeed, income from oil production remained so small during the period of this study that it can be ignored as an important factor in income calculations.

The tables on the following three pages reveal the income

earned in the period 1917 through 1939 from land sales, timber sales, and oil and gas lease payments. The amounts listed represent the most accurate figures that could be obtained from the available sources. In some cases, the handwriting in the old ledger books proved impossible to read. In other instances, several different totals were listed for the same sale; while in some, bookkeepers failed to list the selling price at all or did not distinguish between the gross and net receipts. For all of these reasons, the amounts shown should be considered close approximations only.

Income from Timber Sales, 1917-1939 (values in dollars)

	1917-19	1920-29	1930-39
Brazoria Co.	0.00	0.00	0.00
Brazos Co.	0.00	0.00	0.00
Castro Co.	0.00	0.00	0.00
Grimes Co.	0.00	35,140.50	841.00
Henderson Co.	1,500.00	1,400.00	2,496.44
Houston Co.	0.00	975.00	510.00
Jasper Co.	0.00	0.00	0.00
Leon Co.	0.00	0.00	0.00
Liberty Co.	950.00	9,000.00	8,199.78
Madison Co.	0.00	555.36	4,521.91
Martin Co.	0.00	0.00	0.00
Montgomery Co.	180.00	901.78	310.00
Navarro Co.	0.00	0.00	0.00
Newton Co.	12,468.72	233,881.11	13,146.19
Polk Co.	0.00	0.00	0.00
San Jacinto Co.	36,280.26	18,933.61	21,141.51
Trinity Co.	170,000.00	1,500.00	1.02
Walker Co.	19,224.12	451,044.31	329,299.43

TOTAL	240,603.10	753,331.67	380,467.31

Income from Land Sales, 1917-1939 (values in dollars)

	1917-19	1920-29	1930-39
Brazoria Co.	0.00	0.00	0.00
Brazos Co.	0.00	0.00	0.00
Castro Co.	35,062.50	0.00	0.00
Grimes Co.	1,148.80	444.46	670.00
Henderson Co.	0.00	69.86	157.64
Houston Co.	0.00	0.00	0.00
Jasper Co.	0.00	16.48	59.64
Leon Co.	0.00	449.85	94.60
Liberty Co.	0.00	0.00	0.00
Madison Co.	2,160.68	21,066.53	34,514.30
Martin Co	0.00	0.00	0.00
Montgomery Co.	0.00	62,819.78	7,663.00
Navarro Co.	0.00	0.00	0.00
Newton Co.	4,984.20	3,704.50	18,141.00
Polk Co.	0.00	0.00	0.00
San Jacinto Co.	5,532.28	25,987.01	28,516.92
Trinity Co.	0.00	0.00	0.00
Walker Co.	66,077.29	102,234.13	231,967.06
TOTAL	114,965.75	216,792.60	321,784.16

Income from Oil and Gas Leases, 1917-1939 (values in dollars)

	1917-19	1920-29	1930-39
Brazoria Co.	0.00	20.00	75.00
Brazos Co.	0.00	0.00	0.00
Castro Co.	0.00	0.00	0.00
Grimes Co.	484.24	7,303.17	4,128.93
Henderson Co.	0.00	209.06	19,609.02
Houston Co.	0.00	110.94	2,000.00
Jasper Co.	0.00	0.00	226.38
Leon Co.	0.00	21.00	0.00
Liberty Co.	0.00	1,443.00	5,549.10
Madison Co.	95.45	760.79	3,105.33
Martin Co.	0.00	0.00	0.00
Montgomery Co.	0.00	0.00	27,425.62
Navarro Co.	0.00	0.00	0.00
Newton Co.	0.00	100.00	12,368.35
Polk Co.	0.00	0.00	0.00
San Jacinto Co.	947.44	114,854.63	75,354.93
Trinity Co.	0.00	0.00	0.00
Walker Co.	3,905.10	84,608.44	99,224.36
TOTAL	5,432.23	209,311.03	248,977.02

Note: The information presented in these tables comes from several ledgers, entitled "Inactive Land Book," "Active Land Book," and "Minerals Only Book." All are kept in the Gibbs vault in Huntsville.

For the 1917-1919 period, total earnings from the three sources reached slightly over $360,000.00. With regard to timber sales for the period, the most notable transactions took place in Newton, San Jacinto, Walker, and Trinity counties. Sales in Newton, San

Jacinto, and Walker counties were chiefly to the Palmetto Lumber Company in accordance with the agreements drawn up between the timber company and Sallie Gibbs. The large sale in Trinity County, made to the Rock Creek Lumber Company, consisted of all the marketable pine timber on 1,786 acres. In the land sales category, only one transaction was of a noteworthy nature. The remainder were routine and involved anywhere from ten to one hundred acres. In Castro County, Gibbs Brothers sold its total holding of 2,805 acres in October, 1917, for $35,062.50. This land had been purchased by Sallie Gibbs for speculation purposes in April, 1889. Sallie had paid $2,805.00 for the land. Oil and gas lease payments for the 1917-1919 period formed the smallest of the three income categories. Most of the payments were received for the years 1918 and 1919—that is, during the last year of World War I and the first year of the peace. These figures reflect the local impact of the vitally important oil industry in providing the energy necessary to bring the war to a successful conclusion for the Allied nations. Walker County led in lease income, as it would throughout the period of this study.[10]

In addition to the income shown above, Gibbs Brothers also profited from rents charged those persons who leased company-owned land either for farming purposes or for grazing cattle. As with the other income, it proved exceedingly difficult to obtain precise information on either the amount of land rented or the total earnings from year to year. Enough was available, however, to permit reasonable approximations. For the years 1917-1919 the company rented slightly over 9,000 acres annually, most of which was used for farming. In 1917, land was rented to 259 individuals, forty-seven of whom (19%) were black. In 1918 and 1919, the number of renters totalled 244 and 245, respectively. The percentage of blacks renting land from Gibbs Brothers remained at a nearly constant level, about twenty percent, until the early 1940's, when the company began curtailing the amount of land rented for farming, choosing instead to lease larger tracts for cattle grazing. Profits from land rents for the first three years of company operations came to just under $90,000.00. Additional, though small, earnings came from the rental of mules, wagons, horses, plows, and oxen to the farming tenants.[11]

The bounty provided by the land for the first three years cannot but have kindled a great deal of optimism among the members of the Gibbs family. Since company income derived so substantially from the products of the forests, or from the use of the land, it could only grow as public demand for them expanded. Earnings would increase in direct proportion to any improvements in the material condition of the general population. The return to peacetime conditions following the armistice in November, 1918, enabled the Gibbs family to realize for the first time the considerable economic potential of the lands they held among themselves.

The decade that began on January 1, 1920 was one of the most dramatic in the history of the nation. Following a brief economic downturn in the immediate post-World War I years, the United States entered one of the most prosperous eras it would ever know. By 1921, the domestic economy stood poised for a frenetic burst of growth in virtually all sectors. Two areas that showed particular strength and vitality during the decade were those associated with housing construction and the development of the automobile and related industries, including petroleum.[12]

The most remarkable changes in the Texas economy during the 1920's focused on industrial expansion. The decade witnessed the construction of new manufacturing plants "in record-numbers." Prominent among these were facilities for making commercial use of the products of the East Texas forests as ". . . lumbering became a major industry [during the 1920's], with paper mills employing hundreds of workers and turning out newsprint, wood products, and fine paper . . . ." Milled lumber and other building materials of wood, the traditional products of the Texas forests, also found ready markets, particularly in the housing and commercial construction sectors of the state's economy during the decade.[13]

The growth and development of the timber industry accompanied similar, and sometimes greater, expansion in other areas. Two students of the modern Texas economy have shown that a "spectacular boom of oil activity" overshadowed all other economic advances. The opening of new oil and gas fields in the Panhandle, in North Texas, and in West Texas during the "late teens and early twenties" led to another feverish rush by persons seeking the riches associated with oil. At the end of the decade, the production of petroleum and its products ranked "undoubtedly [as] the greatest factor in the economy of Texas."[14]

As the owner of immense stands of timber and of thousands of acres of land, potentially containing vast oil reserves, Gibbs Brothers and Company was set to profit handsomely from the Twenties Prosperity. True to expectations, the company emerged as the single most important major economic force in Walker and surrounding counties during the 1920's. Income nearly tripled the combined earnings of the previous decade, enabling the managing partners to make some fundamental changes in the structure of company operations. As a result of these transformations, the firm emerged as a more efficient business entity.

Along with the good fortune that accompanied the 1920's, Gibbs family members had to endure great tragedy as well. In late summer, 1921, cancer claimed W. S. Gibbs. W. S. had suffered from the malady for several months, at times fading in and out of consciousness, and always with considerable pain. A few months before his death, he had travelled to Atlantic City, New Jersey, where he could rest and seek recuperation amidst pleasant surroundings that would also permit him quick access to the large medical centers in New York. While there his condition worsened, so he returned to Huntsville. A measure of the esteem and respect W. S. enjoyed among businessmen in the greater Southeast Texas area became apparent when, for the trip back to Huntsville, Robert S. Lovett, chairman of the board of both the Union Pacific and Southern Pacific Railways, made his personal railroad car available to the Gibbs family so that the return trip could be made in greater comfort. W. S. died on September 17, a few weeks before his fifty-fifth birthday.[15]

Following W. S.'s death, the mantle of company leadership passed to T. C. and J. Philip Gibbs, who continued to direct the family firm in accordance with the policies and procedures established when the company was founded. As the older of the two, and having had more experience with the business, T. C. assumed most of the duties previously performed by W. S. He replaced his older brother as president of the Gibbs National Bank and conducted most of the negotiations with the other firms with which Gibbs Brothers and Company did business. T. C. was the only one of the six children of Sandford and Sallie Gibbs to play a prominent, and highly visible, role in Huntsville political affairs. He served as mayor of the town from 1910 through 1913 and during his tenure in office promoted campaigns to pave the city streets and plant pecan trees as part of a city beautification project.[16]

Although the management and governance of Gibbs Brothers and Company remained the same under T. C. and J. Philip Gibbs, the two did not hesitate to place their own stamp on the business. They managed to persuade their siblings to accept changes in the company that would make it more streamlined and better able to focus its attention on the more profitable areas of company activity. The first major change came in 1922, when the Gibbs general mercantile was closed.[17]

From a purely economic point of view, the decision to close the store represented an astute response to the realization that it could no longer compete successfully with the newer types of merchandising establishments. Through the latter decades of the nineteenth century and the early years of the twentieth, Sallie Gibbs had concentrated her attention almost exclusively on the acquisition of land as a base for future family profits. Land potentially offered much greater earnings than did the proceeds from merchandise sales in the general store. Also, by the early 1900's, specialty stores had begun to arrive in Huntsville, making it very difficult for a general mercantile to survive. Retailers that specialized only in dry goods, hardware, feed and grain, drugs and medicines, furniture, men's and women's clothing, or foodstuffs could offer their customers a much greater selection of merchandise, and at better prices, than could a general store that attempted to carry a bit of everything. The fact that the Gibbses decided to close the store, rather than to sell it to someone else who might have wished to try and make it profitable, further supports the contention that it was no longer economically viable.[18]

Within a few months of divesting the family of the store, the two managing partners turned their attention to problems with the Gibbs National Bank. Ever since the establishment of the Huntsville State Bank in 1907, the Gibbses had had to contend with the insidious effects of their rival's advertising. The assertion by Huntsville State that Gibbs National served only the interests of the Gibbs family proved extremely difficult to counter. In point of fact, the Gibbs family did own majority interest in the institution that bore their name, and the suspicion that they used the bank only to enrich themselves further would have come very easily to persons who were already resentful of the financial preeminence of the family. One scholar who grew up in Huntsville has noted that many people in the town viewed the Gibbses as directing a small "faction," made up of their close friends, that sought to control the economic and financial life of the area. Over the years, another faction, made up of individuals from other old families in the town, came together and tried to challenge the Gibbs-controlled group. The Huntsville State Bank was founded by the "other" group that was "not in sympathy with the policies of the National Bank and [was] jealous of their [the Gibbses'] prestige."

> The officers and stock holders [of Huntsville State] were rising professional and business men of the town who did not belong with the "in" group in the other set and evidenced their opposition and dislike in the formation of the new bank . . . with the motto: "The Bank of the People."

The effectiveness of the bank's slogan was such that by early 1920, the Huntsville State Bank, in business only thirteen years, had shown phenomenal growth. Its total assets stood at $587,501.06. At the same time, Gibbs National boasted a total worth of $596,977.72. A third bank in the area, the Riverside State Bank, listed its total holdings at $66,554.35. Faced with such intense competition, the directors at Gibbs National had to devise a tactic to promote their institution. The strategy adopted called for the Gibbs family to sell most of its stock to the public and change the name of the institution to The First National Bank of Huntsville. Accordingly, on January 9, 1923, the name was officially changed and approved by the new stockholders.[19]

The number of shares of First National stock remained at 500, just as had been the case with Gibbs National. Of this number, however, members of the Gibbs family owned only eighty-one, to wit: Dr. J. Philip Gibbs, eleven shares; T. C. Gibbs, ten shares; the estate of W. S. Gibbs, ten shares; and Gibbs Brothers and Company, fifty shares. The remainder of the stock was sold to other individuals, chiefly residents of Huntsville.[20]

In conjunction with the name change, the board members of the First National Bank instituted a different approach in their advertising, hoping to alter the public's perception of the institution. Instead of stressing the safety and security of deposits left in their keeping, as they had done in the past, the board opted to foster the idea that the bank truly cared for each of its patrons. They informed the public that First National was "YOUR BANK, dedicated to your interests." The officers of the bank were "men who know the needs of the community they serve and who are earnestly and honestly striving for the individual success of every customer." The Huntsville State Bank continued to represent itself as "The Bank of the People" and enjoyed an enviable success with its campaign. By late 1925, Huntsville State assets stood at $855,125.54, while First National could claim only $671,854.64.[21] Competition among the banks in Huntsville remained spirited for many years, but by the early 1960's, First National had emerged clearly as the largest in Walker County.[22]

In closing the store and relinquishing control of the bank, T. C. and J. Philip Gibbs hastened the evolution of the family firm to its modern form, i.e. a company whose chief asset is land and whose profits derive from the sale of products from the land or from use of the land by others. The general mercantile of Thomas and Sandford Gibbs had outlived its usefulness. The store had played a vital role in establishing the Gibbs family in Walker County, but by the early decades of the twentieth century, and the arrival of specialty retailing, it had become an anachronism. Had the Gibbs partners decided to invest additional money in the store to resupply and refurbish it to make it competitive, it possibly could have been made a bit more profitable, at least over the short term. The earnings, however, would have remained substantially below those to be made from land and would have become seriously imperiled during the late 1920's and the 1930's, with the emergence of the national chain store retail outlets.

While some element of choice surrounded the decision to

terminate the operations of the mercantile, necessity played the bigger role in altering the family's relationship with the bank. The rapid growth of the Huntsville State Bank, based, at least to some degree, on the widely-held belief that Gibbs National was little more than a financial plaything for the Gibbs family, demanded a forceful and compelling counterstroke. Needed was an action that would convince the public that no individual, or select group of individuals, exerted undue influence in the bank, or profited excessively from bank operations. Yielding majority control of stock ownership constituted a persuasive step in that direction. Even though Gibbs family members would continue through the years to bank at First National, they would never again approach the near-autonomous control they were able to exercise when the institution carried their name.

A little over three years after the birth of the First National Bank, tragedy once again befell the Gibbs family. In mid-February, 1926, while on a business trip to Houston, T. C. suffered a heart attack and died before he could be taken to a hospital. This second untimely death (T. C. was only fifty-six years of age) thrust Dr. J. Philip Gibbs into the role of sole managing partner, a position he would fill until shortly before his death in November, 1965.[23]

The length of Dr. Gibbs's tenure as head of the company enabled him to witness the fruition of all the planning that had begun with Sandford and Sallie Gibbs. During the almost forty years that Dr. Gibbs served as managing partner, Gibbs Brothers enjoyed good times, but suffered through bad as well. Looking over his years as head of the family business, the most enduring tribute to him comes with the realization that under his leadership profits stabilized and a management structure was implemented to perpetuate the successful administrative procedures that had evolved since the company's founding.

For the period 1920-1929, Gibbs Brothers land assets grew by approximately 6,000 acres, from just over 151,000 acres in 1920 to slightly over 157,000 in 1929. The largest gains were registered in San Jacinto and Walker counties, total holdings in each of which increased by roughly 3,000 acres. As the charts on pages 86 through 88 indicate, total earnings for the decade in the three major categories came to just under $1,200,000, a substantial increase over the 1917-1919 period. As in the previous report, timber sales again led all other income categories, with especially good production from Grimes, Newton, San Jacinto, and Walker counties. Continuing contracts with the Palmetto Lumber Company accounted for most of the timber harvest. The considerable increase in receipts from oil and gas leases mirrors the accelerated expansion of all industries, like petroleum, that were ancillary to the rapid growth in the number of automobiles on the roads. During the 1920's, as illustration, the number of vehicles registered and in service rose from roughly two and one-half million to twenty-six and one-half million. For the same period, gasoline production quadrupled and reached a point that it accounted for almost half of all petroleum products refined in the nation.[24]

The majority of land sales during the Twenties were of a routine nature, despite the income figure for Walker County that would appear to indicate otherwise. Overall income totals for the decade were healthy enough that no thought had to be given to reducing the total land holdings. The only noteworthy land transaction occurred in 1924, when Gibbs Brothers sold 5,004 acres in Montgomery County to the Rock Creek Lumber Company for $59,622.00. Evidence suggests that the lumber company wanted the land as a permanent source of timber. Gibbs Brothers retained one-half the mineral interests in the acreage.[25]

Through the 1920's, Gibbs Brothers also continued to rent land to individuals wishing to farm or graze cattle. During the ten year period 1920-1929 an average of 188 persons rented land from the Gibbses annually. The largest number, 233, contracted for the year 1920, while the smallest, 159, obligated themselves for 1928. The steady decline in the number of tenants through the decade represented a trend that would continue until the mid-1930's, when the numbers would increase slightly before beginning a rather precipitate drop late in the decade. The contracts executed between the company and the individual renters were prepared on printed forms, including a careful description of the property, a listing of the rights and responsibilities of each party, and provision for the signatures of at least two witnesses to the agreement. Generally, witnesses were not used. The only exceptions came in the few cases where the renter happened to be illiterate, i.e., unable to read the contract and write his name.[26]

The language of the lease agreements sought to anticipate and resolve potential problems in the execution of the contract. In a typical farm lease, the amount of the rent, be it cash or part of the crop, was stated clearly, as well as the date the rent would fall due. Most payments were to be made by October 1. Additionally, any special conditions were written into the contract. If, for example, a tenant agreed, he could repair fences, clear land, or construct farm buildings to satisfy the rent requirement; and the specific amount of work to be done, along with a division of any costs involved, was put into the agreement. The pasture leases, in addition to spelling out the rental price and the due date, also levied further obligations on the renter. Persons using the land agreed to take care of all fences and structures on the property, to be alert to trespassing, and to help prevent and fight forest fires. Additionally, renters agreed to devote a specified amount of time each year, usually three to four days, to girdling hardwoods so that the dead trees could be removed to make way for additional growth of pine.[27]

As pasture leases began to increase with the decrease in farm tenant agreements in the late 1930's, Gibbs Brothers personnel gave considerable thought to including within the contracts provisions that would afford maximum protection to the land. The switch to cattle raising over farming brought in less revenue from rent, but the lower income was offset in that the cattle were grazed on property that also supported timber. The land, in effect, generated income from two sources. The modified pasture contracts that were worked out over time required that the renter obligate himself to all of the duties found in the earlier tenant agreements: take care of fences, guard against trespassers, and so forth, but additional requirements were also set. Typically, persons leasing pasture land agreed to monitor their animals carefully to make certain that the acreage was not over-grazed and to place only cattle on the land. Additionally, Gibbs Brothers employees, in agreement with the renters, set limits on how many cattle could be placed on each piece of land, prohibited the pasturing of cows with steers so as to control herd size, and stipulated the placement of salt and mineral blocks throughout the pasture to guarantee uniform grazing of the property. Customarily, renters were specifically denied permission to let hogs run on the property as they were considered to be particularly destructive to young pine seedlings.[28]

In renting land to others, Gibbs Brothers agreed to make the property available as stated in the agreement and to abide by all provisions of the contract. It reserved to itself, however, certain rights inherent in the ownership of the land. The company demanded that none of the land be subleased without the approval of Gibbs personnel. Additionally, it maintained the right to sell timber off the land and to permit exploration for oil and gas to take place during the life of the contract. If, in the course of these activities, the renter was denied full use of the land as provided in the contract, an adjustment in the rental price would be worked out.[29]

As nearly as could be determined, Gibbs Brothers earned approximately $60,000 cash, plus 600,000 pounds of cotton for the years 1920-1929. In addition, 129 renters yielded one-third the feed grains and one-fourth of the cotton and cotton seed they produced to pay their rent. The company valued the cotton at twenty cents per pound in 1920. By the mid-1920's, the price had increased to thirty-four cents per pound but by the end of the decade stood just below twenty-cents. The amount of land rented to others during the period grew from approximately 9,000 acres to over 16,000 acres. During the latter half of the decade, there occurred a dramatic increase in the number of persons who rented land by pledging one-fourth the cotton and one-third the feed grains, with a corresponding reduction in the number of people paying a fixed cash sum for rent. For the years 1920-1925, fewer than ten persons a year paid their rent by dividing their crops according to a pre-arranged formula. Beginning in 1926, the number jumped to twenty-five and remained at that level, or higher, for well over a decade. The abrupt change represented a reaction by the company to the general decline in agricultural commodity prices, particularly in reference to cotton, that began in the late 1920's. The drop in cotton values, which continued unabated through the Depression years of the 1930's, convinced many farmers that they could not afford to obligate themselves for a set cash sum each year, hence the decision to share their production to satisfy the rent requirements. For its part, Gibbs Brothers accepted the reductions in income that accompanied crop division rather than have the lands lie fallow and produce nothing.[30]

The general uncertainty in the agricultural sector of the nation's economy during the late 1920's presaged the severe and prolonged economic downturn that followed the collapse of the stock market in 1929. The hard times of the 1930's affected Texas much as they did the rest of the country. Industrial production, though still in its infancy in the state, fell off drastically, prices for goods and services declined, and unemployment, which generated a pervasive and searing bounty of human misery and suffering, became commonplace. Private and governmental relief efforts provided limited, though important, assistance, but much more was needed in a state like Texas, with an economy almost wholly dependent on agriculture and petroleum. During the 1930's, prices for cotton, the major agricultural staple, and oil fell to unprecedented levels. Cotton fell to less than five or six cents per pound, well below the cost of production, and the value of oil dropped to as low as eight cents per barrel.[31]

Amidst economic turmoil of such a magnitude, it was inevitable that the Depression would have a profound impact on every level of society, even the most financially secure. A check of the three major Gibbs Brothers income categories for the years 1930-1939 reveals that earnings during the period dropped by nearly a quarter of a million dollars, with further losses occurring in the farm rents. Timber revenues constituted the largest single area of decline—occasioned, no doubt, by a significant drop in demand for lumber that accompanied the drastic curtailment of all types of construction during the decade. Oil and gas lease income registered a slight increase over the 1920's level, with most payments received during 1938 and 1939, as the economy began to experience the beginnings of recovery. Earnings from farm rents declined to just over $50,000 cash and 300,000 pounds of cotton. During the years 1930-1935, the company received an average of approximately 40,000 pounds of cotton per year. Beginning in 1936, however, and continuing through 1939, cotton receipts dropped to less than 18,000 pounds per year. Much of the land that had formerly been used to cultivate cotton was permitted to remain idle or was converted to pasture. An average of 181 persons rented land from the Gibbses annually during the 1930's, with three hundred of the total number pledging part of their crops as rent, in accordance with the one-fourth, one-third formula.

Further evidence of the degree to which the company had to adjust to reduced circumstances during the decade is illustrated by the fact that thirty-one renters took care of their rent obligations by performing some chore, such as repairing fences, digging wells, etc., and an average of thirty-five persons each year paid total rents of less than ten dollars.[32]

The dramatic decline in tenant farming on Gibbs land that began in the late 1930's mirrored similar developments in the rest of the state and throughout the South. Federal government farm programs, whether through the Agricultural Adjustment Administration (AAA) or the later Soil Conservation and Domestic Allotment Act, sought to reduce and stabilize agricultural production. This resulted in fewer people farming land for others and the conversion to a wage labor system to replace tenantry. The industrialization and manufacturing growth that accompanied the conversion to a wartime economy in the early 1940's also helped end tenant farming in that it provided employment options to the renters that were previously unavailable. And finally, the intense competition from the emerging cotton producing counties in West Texas, where farm size was much larger and mechanization commonplace, rendered the small tenant farms in the eastern part of the state economically obsolete. By the mid-1930's, perceptive agricultural observers could see the coming changes and could recognize that "the old system of tenantry is doomed . . . ."[33]

The economic hardship of the 1930's, as reflected in the dramatic decline in farm income, led company leaders to focus renewed attention on the land and its earning potential. Of particular importance were the timber holdings, with special concern directed toward determining their general health and their ability, over the long term, to produce the kinds of revenues the family wanted. Out of this intense scrutiny and evaluation came the realization that more progressive policies would have to be adopted that would protect and sustain the vitality and productivity of the forests. The innovations in forest management the company would eventually adopt would reverse traditional practice and give primary emphasis to the protection of timberland resources. The company would have to become better stewards of the land in order to guarantee continuing productivity.

From its very beginnings, lumbering in the United States had practiced clearcutting as the most common form of timber extraction. Loggers would move into an area of virgin timber and remove all marketable trees, leaving the area essentially without young, healthy stock to replenish the losses. Starting in the northeastern parts of the nation, the lumber companies moved slowly westward to the enormous timber stands around the Great Lakes and then into the South following the Civil War. By the time professional logging reached eastern Texas, axes and animal-driven machinery had given way to more efficient crosscut saws and steam-powered equipment, both of which greatly speeded the process of clearing an area of forest. One description of the aftermath of an early twentieth century lumbering operation in Texas has painted an appalling picture:

> When a logging operation finished with an area it was left desolated. The area was littered with broken and twisted tops and dotted with stumps. A few pines were left because they had been too small or crooked; they had survived damage from the skidders, other falling trees, or the fires which usually swept the area following the logging operations. From these few seed trees a few seedlings came up, usually only to fall victim to hogs, goats, cattle, fires, erosion or disease. The few that survived were not enough to replenish the forests.[34]

The denuding of the forestlands also brought unanticipated and even more environmentally damaging results:

> With the destruction of the forest come periods of great drouth . . . followed by excessive floods. When the trees are gone, the forest floor and forest litter dries and burns up. This, in the woodland, is always wet and gives birth to springs and rivulets. Floods now rush unchecked over vast areas of the best farming land, washing its fertility into the creeks and rivers causing disastrous overflow.[35]

The rapidly deteriorating condition of Texas forests engaged the attention of leading East Texas businessmen during the early years of this century and, in 1915, the establishment of a state forest service received legislative approval. For the ensuing several decades, forest service personnel conducted education seminars and presentations seeking to convince landowners and the public of the need for reforestation, fire protection, insect control, and other programs that could protect the timber resources. Proper management of forests could guarantee a constant and easily renewable natural resource that would greatly enrich the entire state. All of the attention paid to the forests as a long-term, dependable source of lumber convinced Gibbs Brothers personnel to reconsider their timber management policies.[36]

Beginning in the late 1930's, company officers began to consider a variety of alternative forest management policies and eventually adopted what would become known as selection timber management. In essence, company foresters began to think of the timber holdings as long-term investments which, if handled properly, would permit sizable annual withdrawals and yet leave enough trees to provide for future needs. Each year only the adult, mature trees, those beyond their reproductive prime, would be cut, removed, and sold. Removal of the mature timber would make room for the younger trees to grow and develop so that they could be harvested in the future. The new policy possessed the further environmental advantage of guaranteeing that the land would always be covered with healthy stands of timber that would protect and enrich the soil, prevent erosion and rainwater runoff, provide shelter for wildlife, and contribute significantly to the aesthetic value of the region.[37]

The growing concern for the health and vitality of the state's forests during the early decades of the twentieth century did not bring an immediate end to the ecological ravages associated with clearcutting. Many of the large lumber companies, especially those that owned their own timber stands, continued to harvest as they always had, by removing all trees in a particular section of land. Following the harvest the companies would then go back in, replant the area with seedling trees, and wait for them to mature and reach merchantable size. Gibbs Brothers, on the other hand, has maintained its commitment to selection management. Environmental concerns aside—and these are not inconsiderable among Gibbs partners and management—the company has never been able to afford the very high costs associated with clearcutting. Since Gibbs Brothers is not, and never has been, a lumber company, it does not own sawmills and thus cannot earn the extra profit that comes from selling the finished lumber; it cannot support the long-term costs required to nurture and care for the young trees, plus pay all the land taxes, for the twenty or twenty-five years required for a new crop of trees to mature. Company lands must produce revenue annually or they become an intolerable economic burden that drains financial resources away from other income areas.[38]

The only income category to show substantial growth during the 1930's, that of land sales, came about primarily because of several profitable transactions in Madison, Newton, San Jacinto, and Walker counties. Evidence indicates that at some point early in the decade, a decision was made to sell some of the company lands to offset losses in other income areas. Additional motivation for a sale arose from the difficulties the company was encountering in overseeing and protecting its interests in landholdings located at considerable distance from Walker County. By selling off the lands in some of the more distant areas, the company could begin to consolidate its holdings in and around Huntsville, where it could better administer the property and, perhaps, make it more productive.

The sales in Newton County were made in 1936 and 1938 and involved the transfer of just under 3,000 acres. The land had been bought in the first decade of the twentieth century as part of the agreement with the Palmetto Lumber Company, but in the years since the purchase substantial quantities of the merchantable timber had been removed. The first of the transactions took place on November 14, 1936, and consisted of the sale of 2,023.5 acres to Messrs. Morgan, Lindsey, and Lindsey of Jasper, Texas. The three men paid a total of $12,141.00 for the land, which translated to six dollars per acre. Gibbs Brothers retained the right to one-half of all future mineral royalties, as well as one-half the proceeds of all mineral leases. The buyers, for their part, agreed to respect and make no claims on the mineral leases Gibbs Brothers had already arranged.[39]

A little over eighteen months after the sale to the Jasper men, the company arranged another transaction. The latter deal, concluded on June 9, 1938, called for the sale of 848.3 acres in Newton County to the Weir Longleaf Lumber Company of Houston. Weir paid $6,000 for the land (slightly over seven dollars per acre) and agreed that Gibbs Brothers would retain a one-half interest in all minerals and mineral leases executed on the land. The Gibbses also reserved the right of free access to the property for purposes of exploration and extraction of minerals, but agreed to pay a fair market price for any timber damaged in the process of a mineral search or removal.[40]

In addition to the land sales in Newton County, Gibbs Brothers also parted with substantial acreage in Madison County. Records indicate that none of the latter transactions was of a particularly noteworthy nature. The company simply found opportunities to unload some acreage profitably and took advantage of them. Most of the Madison County sales occurred between 1935 and 1938.[41]

The two largest sales, those that generated the greatest amount of income, took place in 1935 and 1939, respectively, and involved the transfer of just over 30,000 acres to the United States Government. Once under federal control, the acreage became the Sam Houston National Forest. In all, the federal government during the 1930's established four national forests in Texas: the Sam Houston, Davy Crockett, Angelina, and Sabine.[42]

An early historian of the lumbering industry in Texas has written that the movement to establish national forests in the state began in 1934, "when the state legislature invited the federal government to set up one or more national forests . . . as part of its conservation and employment programs." The purposes of the forests in the state centered around rescuing areas where the original timber had been damaged, burned, or clearcut. The areas would be replanted and the young trees nurtured carefully so as to provide "timber reserves to insure against a shortage . . . ." In addition, the forests would be available for public recreation, would serve as laboratories for "forestry experimentation and demonstration," and would protect vital watersheds.[43]

The lands that formed the Sam Houston National Forest were purchased from three firms: the Delta Land and Timber Company, the Foster Lumber Company, and Gibbs Brothers, which, although not a lumber company, nonetheless owned considerable timber acreage in the areas designated by the state forester to be included in the new forest. Immediately prior to the purchase, representatives from the United States Forest Service inspected Gibbs-owned lands in the area of the new federal forest and appraised their value. The federal agents then selected which of the lands they wanted and arranged for new surveys to be done. Gibbs Brothers had no say in selecting which acreage the federal government chose to buy. Upon completion of the resurveys, Gibbs personnel and federal representatives agreed upon a price for the land and the arrangement was concluded. In December, 1935, the company sold 25,204 acres and in August, 1939, an additional 5,246.3 acres, making a total of 30,450.3, roughly one-fifth of the total acreage in the national forest. The average price for the land came to just under $7.50 per acre. With the exception of 817 acres in Montgomery County, all of the land sold to the federal government was situated in San Jacinto and Walker counties.[44]

As part of the contract of sale to the federal government, Gibbs Brothers and Company retained title to all minerals "in, on, and under" the land until January 1, 2037. In working out the terms and conditions for any future mineral leases or mining, the company and the government arrived at a set of procedures that sought to protect the rights of the company while at the same time insuring that the natural integrity of the forest would be maintained. The following list contains the principal provisions of the procedures governing mineral leases and removal that appeared in both agreements between the United States Government and Gibbs Brothers and Company. They are worth noting to the degree that they foreshadow a concern for the protection of the natural environment that would not become publicly popular until many years later.

1. All persons prospecting or mining the land must have the permission of Gibbs Brothers and Company and must follow procedures established by the U.S. Department of Agriculture.

2. All mining and prospecting operations must be open to federal inspection to guarantee that they comply with federal requirements and that the surface of the land is respected.

3. All mining and prospecting must be done under procedures that protect the purity of nearby streams and rivers, and hydraulic

mining is strictly prohibited.

4. No timber may be cut, or destroyed, as an incident to mineral exploration or extraction without the permission of the United States Government. In those cases where permission is given to cut or destroy timber, the U.S. Government must be paid for the trees at the prevailing market rate.

5. All buildings, roads, bridges, etc., necessary for the exploration and extraction of minerals must be approved by government representatives and placed only in locations in which the U.S. Government concurs. Any debris left at the site after exploration or extraction have been completed must be disposed of in accordance with U.S. Government procedures. All buildings and tools not removed from the site within six months of completion of exploration or extraction become the property of the U.S. Government.

6. Any hazardous materials generated by mineral exploration or extraction must be disposed of in accordance with U.S. Government procedures.

7. All persons engaged in mineral exploration or extraction must use proper diligence to prevent forest fires; must help extinguish forest fires that break out in their mining locality; and will be held responsible for fires they cause.

8. On January 1, 2037, the mineral rights on the land become the property of the United States Government. If, however, at that time Gibbs Brothers is producing commercial quantities of minerals, the extraction rights will extend for five more years on those units already producing, or within an area one-eighth mile from a producer.[45]

There can be no doubt that the sale of land to the federal government came about, to some degree at least, because of the near-distress conditions in which the company found itself in the 1930's. Declining revenues in the first half of the decade, coupled with the forbidding prospect of an interminable period of economic depression, persuaded the partners in the firm that the sale had to be made. By retaining the mineral rights, company officials hoped to compensate somewhat for the certain losses they would incur from being denied future timber harvests from the land. Put very simply, company officials found themselves in a very difficult financial position and worked out the best deal they could under the circumstances. In addition to the economic problems with which they had to contend during the 1930's, Gibbs family members suffered the loss of Sarah Sandford Gibbs Norsworthy. Known as "Tantie" by her several nieces and nephews, Mrs. Norsworthy died on November 27, 1933, in San Antonio. She left no heirs, but instructed that her share of the family partnership holdings be divided among the several grandchildren of Sandford and Sallie Gibbs.[46]

As the 1930's drew to a close, the nation continued to suffer from the malignant effects of the Depression. The many public assistance programs put into effect by the federal government had helped ease the suffering somewhat, but had not restored the nation's economic health as many had hoped and prophesied. In Texas, per capita income at the end of the decade remained depressed, while the number of people working on relief remained high. President Roosevelt's New Deal, despite its good intentions and concern for the economically helpless, had neither ended the Depression nor brought recovery. The Gibbs family, although it continued to occupy a much more privileged financial position than did the majority of Walker County citizens, nonetheless had had to retrench and lower its level of economic expectations. The significant decline in earnings during the decade had forced the family to take drastic steps to forestall even greater losses. The sales of land during the 1930's, spurred by the need to generate income and maintain liquidity, had resulted in a reduction of over 36,000 acres in total landholdings, roughly one-fourth of the amount held at the beginning of the decade. The income realized from these sales formed a substantial part of the foundation upon which the future of the company would be based.[47]

The Depression came to an end amidst the manufacturing and industrial boom that accompanied America's entry into World War II. All major industries geared themselves to war production, while the mobilization of manpower to work in the factories and enlist in the armed forces virtually ended unemployment. The domestic economy grew at an astonishing rate during the war years and firmly re-established the nation's economic and industrial dominance. When the war ended, in late summer 1945, the country was poised to enter the most prosperous period of its history and Gibbs Brothers, with its financial foundation firmly based in land ownership, was poised to take full advantage of the coming economic bonanza. The post-World War II decades would bring profit and prosperity to Gibbs Brothers that would far exceed any dreams, wishes, or expectations that might have been entertained by Sandford or Sallie Gibbs.

AFTERWORD

In 1991, Gibbs Brothers celebrated its sesquicentennial year of doing business. The American society and economy have changed much since 1841, and the company has grown and flourished along with the state and the nation. Despite the many changes, however, in one very important area things have remained much the same. Beginning with Thomas and Sandford Gibbs and continuing through the officers of recent years, Gibbs Brothers has charted an essentially conservative course. It has maintained its economic base in land ownership and has devoted most of its creative energies to devising ways of making the land more productive. Over the last half century or so, company revenues have exceeded by a considerable margin any earnings for a similar period in the firm's history. Recent profit levels stand as convincing testimony to the wisdom of adhering to policies that seek a steady and patient growth and that are securely rooted in a profound appreciation of the land and a keen understanding of its productive potential.

In the years following World War II, Gibbs family members experienced the deaths of all of the remaining children of Sandford and Sallie Gibbs. Mary Alla Gibbs Robinson died in 1958 at the age of ninety. Seven years later, and also after reaching his ninetieth year, Dr. J. Philip Gibbs passed away, and in 1976, Luteola Gibbs Hawley, the youngest child, died at her home in Dallas. She was ninety-eight.[1]

Each of the deaths placed a great strain on those who remained behind trying to protect the company from any financial reversals that might ensue. Their task was made much easier, however, by some management restructuring completed by Dr. Gibbs and the other partners in 1961. Indeed, by the time the mantle of leadership passed to the younger generation in the mid-1960's, the family and the firm had not only established themselves as solid, highly-respected members of the community—they had also put in place a governing structure designed to provide for an orderly transfer of leadership while maintaining long-standing company traditions. By virtually any measure, Gibbs Brothers stood among the more progressive, civic-minded groups within Walker County and maintained its support for a wide range of educational and community improvement projects and programs, thus perpetuating the commitment begun by Thomas and Sandford Gibbs during the early years of the nineteenth century.

Late in his life, as he considered the long-term well-being and stability of Gibbs Brothers, Dr. Gibbs, working with company attorneys, sought to implement policy changes that would safeguard the Gibbs partnership arrangement into the future. At issue were the twin questions of how to provide for an orderly succession after all of the six children of Sandford and Sallie, the original founders of the firm, had passed from the scene and also how to prevent some partner in the future from trying to partition out his or her assets and, in the process, weaken or diminish the strength of the remain-ing partnership holdings. Of the two, the question touching on the stability of company assets ranked as the more worrisome.

In the years after World War II, and concomitant to the prosperity of the times, the market value of Gibbs landholdings increased substantially over pre-war levels and would continue to grow as population increases in the state created a demand for land. Projecting into the future, family members realized that later generations of Gibbses might well grow up in cities and towns far removed from Huntsville and thus have little awareness of the value and diversity of the family holdings or of the absolute necessity for keeping the lands intact as a single economic unit. In a scenario of the worst case, a future partner might find himself in extreme financial distress and be tempted to seek relief, or have his creditors do so for him, by demanding that his share of the company assets be separated from the whole so that they could be sold at whatever the market would bring to retire any indebtedness. Such a demand would force the remaining partners to hire attorneys to protect their own interests and, in the process of seeking an equitable division of the assets, a virtually impossible task to accomplish, all would spend large amounts of money and destroy whatever there was of family unity and cohesion.[2]

After much thought, discussion, and debate, family members came up with feasible solutions to the two problems. On the matter of a successor to Dr. Gibbs, they decided to establish a collective leadership for the firm. As it evolved, a representative from each of the five Gibbs families—i.e., the descendants of each of the five original Gibbs offspring who left heirs—would sit as a member of a company executive committee and would decide the broad outlines of company policy. From among the five representatives, one individual, to be called senior partner, would be elected to serve as titular head of the firm and carry out the decisions of the executive committee. In its essence, the committee arrangement simply perpetuated, albeit in a more formal structure, the governance policies that had been in effect since the founding of the company. Whereas previously the managing partners had been able to consult informally with their siblings prior to making major decisions, the sheer growth in the number of partners through the years rendered such casual arrangements impossible. An executive committee, with each branch of the family having equal representation in company decisions and commensurate responsibility for their success, constituted the only practical form in which the collectivity of leadership could be maintained and, at the same time, preserve the continuity of company tradition.[3]

To blunt the potential threat of a family member's trying to partition company assets, the partners decided to impose further restrictions on themselves, thereby making any such eventuality most unlikely. In a legal agreement dated October 1, 1961, the partners laid down very specific terms and conditions under which any sale of individual assets could proceed. The agreement contained two major provisions, the first of which required that a partner wishing to sell his interest, that is, his share of the landholdings in the firm, make written notification of such to all the other partners who would then have first option to buy the interest offered for sale. Secondly, the interest could not be sold for a price higher than its "book" value. The agreement defined the book value as the original cost of the property, less "any reserves for depreciation, and less all debts, obligations and liabilities" associated with it. By 1961, the book value of the company lands, most of which had been purchased many years earlier when land values were low, stood substantially below their prevailing market value. Thus, any partner who persisted in selling his interest would, in the process, do himself a serious financial disservice. The agreement did not prohibit any of the partners from giving his share of the company holdings to someone else, but did stipulate that the recipient "shall receive such interest subject to all terms of the Partnership Agreement as amended."[4]

There can be no doubt but that the management changes instituted by the Gibbs descendants just before the death of Dr. Gibbs greatly strengthened the partnership arrangement. Indeed, the continuing success of the firm into the present era can be explained, to a large degree, by the partners agreeing to bind themselves even closer together and maintain their land holdings as a single unit. The size and extent of Gibbs property ownership, and the strength with which it is bound together, protects the individual partners from financial calamity and enables company leaders to negotiate with other firms from a near-unassailable financial position.

Another factor that has helped in building success for Gibbs Brothers has been the company's commitment to use its financial strength and position in ways that benefit the entire area. From the very beginning, Thomas and Sandford Gibbs lent their influence to all worthy projects that would promote the orderly development of their town and county. Whether it be attracting railroads to the area, supporting local educational and religious institutions, assisting state agencies when help was critical, or any of a variety of other local efforts, the Gibbses have been in the vanguard of those forces seeking the constant improvement of life in Walker County. For a great many years, they have been the first source local people turned to for help and leadership in civic improvement campaigns. In the words of one long-time resident, "Anyone working in behalf of a worthy cause could go to the Gibbses and be assured of support of some kind, either financial or moral, or, most often, both."[5]

The role played by the Gibbses through the years in fostering growth and development in Walker County places them squarely among those economic and business elites that have guided much of the South's development since the end of the Civil War. As a number of recent scholars have noted, local civic leaders enthusiastically supported innovations and reforms aimed at attracting new business and industry to an area. They promoted the building of economic and transportation infrastructures and sought to refashion local politics to promote greater efficiency and responsibility. These civic elites throughout the South embraced a progressive ethos, the central core of which included "the necessity for growth and order, change and stability, progress and preservation." The leadership of these elites came most often from the middle and upper classes in a particular town or region and typically made their contributions to civic improvement through "voluntary civic organizations" that helped fund "existing religious and charitable agencies," along with other worthy undertakings. Local chambers of commerce and industry rank as the most important of all these voluntary organizations in that they "appropriated to themselves the task of defining and encouraging general community growth and well-being."[6]

These Southern civic-commercial elites often engaged in a type of aggressive boosterism designed to publicize the good features of their town and, at the same time, generate enthusiasm among their fellow townsmen for further improvements to keep their cities in the forefront of progressive development. During the early decades of the twentieth century, few topics excited the interest of civic boosters as much as did the arrival of the automobile. Motorized travel promised to link towns and cities and rural and urban areas with a speed and ease that would transform all of society. Everyone recognized the enormous benefit that could be derived from the automobile and sought to make certain that "roads, highways, and related facilities could be provided rapidly enough to insure the maximum degree of economic advantage [to the local area]." Street construction and improvement, projects within the purview of local political control, "constituted the single most time-consuming item on the agendas of southern city governments" during much of the early twentieth century. T. C. Gibbs's efforts on behalf of street paving during his term as mayor of Huntsville in the early 1920's, continuing the many years of civic leadership begun by Thomas and Sandford

Gibbs, merely affirms this long-standing family tradition and further emphasizes the commitment the Gibbs family has made to the development of their town and county and locates them firmly among the progressive-minded, forward-looking Southern leaders of their time.[7]

In the particular case of the Gibbses, their unique position as the preeminent economic power in Walker and surrounding counties places a special importance on all of their actions. Any mistakes they make will have the greatest adverse effect on them and their holdings. The public responsibilities that accompany their financial position are taken very seriously by the partners in the Gibbs firm. Members of the company executive committee identify closely with the town of Huntsville and recognize very clearly that as the owners of the largest blocks of land in the area they stand to lose the most if they pursue policies that hinder or impede progress. For this reason, what might be termed "the impact on Walker County" figures prominently in all company deliberations.

Nothing better illustrates the happy coincidence of combining profits with concern for the greater benefit of the local area than does the decision in the early 1940's to follow the precepts of selection management in Gibbs timber holdings. As was noted earlier, selection management enables timber owners to reap an annual harvest of their trees but to do so in a manner that leaves large stands of timber untouched, thus maintaining animal habitat, watershed and soil erosion protection, recreational opportunities, and so forth, all the benefits generally associated with healthy forests. During the last half-century or so, Gibbs timber management practices have rescued many acres of "cut-over" forestland, severely damaged by clearcutting, and have restored them, in the words of one observer, to "beautiful, profitable forests . . . ." East Texas forest ecologists and environmentalists alike have been quick to salute Gibbs Brothers for its environmentally sound practices and have used the family operation as an example to show other timber growers and lumber companies that selection management can indeed be profitable and at the same time environmentally friendly.[8]

Additional evidence of the way in which Gibbs Brothers' normal business operations can bring profit to the company as well as benefit to the region can be seen in the results of a recent decision to permit the Louisiana-Pacific Company (formerly Georgia-Pacific) to harvest Gibbs timber. Even though the date of the agreement falls outside the time limit of this study, it bears at least brief examination for what it reveals of the company attitude toward progress and development. The contract with Louisiana-Pacific represented the culmination of efforts by the lumber company to locate dependable supplies of timber for its mills, and by Gibbs Brothers to find long-term arrangements that would bring better prices for its marketable trees. The agreement between the two firms, signed on September 24, 1969, called for Louisiana-Pacific to harvest adult trees from some 77,000 acres of Gibbs-owned land in Walker, Madison, San Jacinto, and Grimes counties. Among its more important provisions, the agreement listed the types and sizes of trees to be cut and limited the yearly harvest of the trees that fit the size specifications, thus insuring that there would always be dense stands of timber on the lands. Nothing in the contract prevented Louisiana-Pacific from purchasing trees from other local landowners so that, in effect, the favorable prices Gibbs Brothers negotiated for its timber became the standard for all timber sales from other owners in the area. A further benefit from the agreement with Louisiana-Pacific came when the lumber company announced it was going to build a sawmill just south of Huntsville to process the timber harvested in the area. The mill began operations in 1971, providing employment to over four hundred persons.[9]

The fact that Gibbs Brothers could offer long-term access to many thousands of acres of timber played an important part in the negotiations with Louisiana Pacific. Having been assured of dependable supplies of saw logs over an extended period, the lumber company could invest in the construction of a mill, with the reasonable expectation that long-term profits from local operations would help it recoup its initial outlays. Being able to negotiate with a single management team, like the one at Gibbs Brothers, that controlled large acreage saved considerable time and confusion in contract talks. The final agreement would have been much more difficult to reach had the lumber company been forced to negotiate with a large number of smaller landowners, who likely could not have reached a consensus as to either price or length of cutting contract.[10]

The contract with Louisiana-Pacific stands as convincing evidence of the crucial advantage the company has held through the years by virtue of the size of its landholdings. It is no exaggeration to say that maintaining the total holdings intact is absolutely essential to future success. Managing its lands as a single unit will give company leaders a decided edge in all future negotiations with other firms. The lesson to be learned from the "bundle of sticks" story—whether it be apocryphal or not—remains as valid today as it was over three quarters of a century ago.

Notes

Preface and Acknowledgements:

[1]*Huntsville Item,* 15 January 1964, 8.

[2]Lynn A. Mason, Texas Historical Commission, to the author, 29 August 1985.

[3]Lewis E. Atherton, "The Pioneer Merchant in Mid-America," *The University of Missouri Studies* XIV, No. 2, (1 April 1939), *passim.*

[4]______. *The Southern Country Store, 1800-1860* (Baton Rouge: Louisiana State University Press, 1949), *passim.*

[5]Thomas D. Clark, *Pills, Petticoats and Plows: The Southern Country Store* (New York: Bobbs-Merrill Company, 1944), *passim.*

[6]*Ibid.*, 13 and 313-336.

[7]John Stricklin Spratt, *The Road to Spindletop: Economic Change in Texas, 1875-1901* (Austin: University of Texas Press, 1970), *passim;* Edmund Miller, "A Financial History of Texas," *Bulletin of the University of Texas* (1916), *passim.*

Introduction:

[1]Writers' Program of the Works Projects Administration in the State of Texas, American Guide Series, *Texas: A Guide to the Lone Star State,* (New York: Hastings House, Publishers, 1940), 417.

[2]Mrs. Davis Cox, *Historic Huntsville, Texas: Its Growth and Progress for Sixty-Two Years from 1837 to 1899* (n.p.: n.p., 1899), 3.

[3]John W. Baldwin, "An Early History of Walker County, Texas" (M. A. thesis, Sam Houston State Teachers College, 1957), 9-25; D'Anne McAdams Crews, editor and compiler, *Huntsville and Walker County, Texas: A Bicentennial History* (Huntsville: Sam Houston State University Press, 1976), 5-49.

[4]Baldwin, "Early History of Walker County, Texas," 5-49; David M. Vigness, *The Revolutionary Decades: The Saga of Texas, 1810-1836* (Austin: Steck-Vaughn Company, 1965), 93-110; Eugene C. Barker, *The Life of Stephen F. Austin, Founder of Texas, 1793-1836: A Chapter in the Westward Movement of the Anglo-American People* (Austin: University of Texas Press, 1969), 178-230; William C. Binkley, *The Texas Revolution* (Baton Rouge:

Louisiana State University Press, 1952), 1-35; Paul Lack, *The Texas Revolutionary Experience: A Political and Social History 1835-1836* (College Station: Texas A&M University Press, 1992), vi-xxv.

[5]Vigness, *Revolutionary Decades*, 93-110; Barker, *Life of Stephen F. Austin,* 256-266 and 322-369; Lack, *Texas Revolutionary Experience,* 3-8.

[6]Vigness, *Revolutionary Decades*, 173-198; Llerena Friend, *Sam Houston, The Great Designer* (Austin: University Of Texas Press, 1969), 56-69; Lack, *Texas Revolutionary Experience,* 96-104.

[7]Wilbourn Sandford Gibbs, "The Gibbs Family Beginnings in Union County," in *Union County Heritage, 1981*, Mannie Lee Mabry, ed. (n. p.: Union County Heritage Committee, 1981), 103-104; Wilbourn Sandford Gibbs, "Genealogy of the Descendants of Hiram Gibbs," 1-5.

[8]Gibbs, "Genealogy of Descendants of Hiram Gibbs," 3-5.

Chapter I:

[1]Gibbs, "Gibbs Family Beginnings in Union County," 103.

[2]Lewis Atherton, "Itinerant Merchandising in the Ante-bellum South," *Bulletin of the Business Historical Society* Vol. XIX (1945), 35-57.

[3]Mary Austin Holley, *Texas* (Austin: The Texas State Historical Association, 1985), 1.

[4]*Ibid.*, 15.

[5]*Ibid.*, 15-20.

[6]*Ibid.*, 22-23.

[7]*Ibid.*, 109-125.

[8]Mrs. E. M. Houstoun (Matilda Charlotte), *Texas and the Gulf of Mexico: Or, Yachting in the New World* (Austin: Steck-Warlick Company, 1968), 126-136, 192-211.

[9]Frederick Law Olmsted, *A Journey Through Texas, or, A Saddle-Trip on the Southwestern Frontier* (Austin: University of Texas Press, 1978), 46-108.

[10]1841 Daybook, Gibbs Brothers and Company, 1, 27, 62, 159, and 201. All of the ledgers, journals, and daybooks used in this manuscript are the property of Gibbs Brothers and Company and are housed in the company vault in Huntsville.

[11]*Ibid.*, 157 and 217; Deed from Pleasant and Hannah Gray to Thomas Gibbs and Gardner R. Coffin, 11 October 1842, Gibbs Brothers and Company.

[12]1841 Daybook, 100; Deed from Nathan Coffin to Thomas Gibbs, 10 June

1844; Agreement between Thomas Gibbs and Sandford St. John Gibbs, 20 July 1847. Both the deed and the agreement are housed in the vault of Gibbs Brothers and Company.

[13]Walker County Tax Roll, 1846.

[14]1841 Daybook, 1-50.

[15]1841 Daybook, *passim;* 1847 Daybook, *passim.*

[16]1841 Daybook, 1-15.

[17]*Ibid., passim.*

[18]*Ibid.*, 1, 3, 8, 15, and 18.

[19]The two examples related come from Louis J. Wortham, *A History of Texas* V, 211-212, quoted in Hamilton P. Easton, "The History of the Texas Lumbering Industry" (Ph.D. dissertation, University of Texas at Austin, 1947), 75-78.

[20]Gibbs to A.G. Dumicer, 16 August 1860, Gibbs Letterpress; L.B. Hightower account, 1860 Daybook, 236.

[21]1841 Daybook, *passim*; 1848 Daybook, *passim.*

[22]Atherton, *Southern Country Store,* 49-54; Fred Mitchell Jones, *Middlemen in the Domestic Trade of the United States, 1800-1860* (Urbana: University of Illinois, 1937), 44-45.

[23]Gibbs to Trowbridge Dwight Co., 18 May 1860, Gibbs Letterpress; Gibbs to I. T. Moore Co., 13 June 1860, Gibbs Letterpress.

[24]Thomas D. Clark, *Pills, Petticoats, and Plows: The Southern Country Store* (New York: The Bobbs-Merrill Company, 1944), 76-124 and 313-336; 1862 Daybook, 1457.

[25]Donald R. Walker, *Penology for Profit: A History of the Texas Prison System, 1867-1912* (College Station: Texas A&M University Press, 1988), 24-27.

[26]*Ibid.*, 16-17.

[27]*Ibid.*, 28-31 and 169-171.

[28]*Ibid.*, 49-53.

[29]1848 Daybook, 647. Kersey is a coarse woolen cloth used for work clothes. A roundabout is a short, close-fitting jacket popular with men and boys in the nineteenth century. Cottonade is a heavy, coarse twilled cotton fabric used for work clothes. A hickory shirt is one made of a strong twilled cotton fabric, used especially for work clothes. Brogans are work shoes made of coarse leather and reaching to the ankle.

[30]1848 Daybook, *passim;* 1852 Daybook, *passim.*

[31]1862 Daybook, 1516-1522; Gibbs to T.W. House Co., 14 May 1860;

Gibbs to E.W. Cawthon, 3 July 1860; Gibbs to I. T. Westmoreland Company, Danville, Illinois, 3 July 1860; Gibbs to Jacquer and Byrd and Co., 22 October 1860; Gibbs to William Marsh Rice Co., 6 November 1860, Gibbs Letterpress.

[32]Contract between T&S Gibbs and D.C. Dickson, Financial Agent of the Texas Penitentiary, 13 November 1866. Contract housed in the Penitentiary Papers, Archives Division, Texas State Library, Austin, Texas.

[33]Pleasant Williams Kittrell, *The Kittrell Journal* (Bryan, Texas: Family History Foundation, 1980), 189, 209, and 247.

[34]1841 Daybook, *passim*; 1848 Daybook, *passim*; 1860 Daybook, *passim*; Will of Sam Houston, Book D, Probate Minutes, Walker County, Texas, 613.

[35]Gibbs to McLain and Buckley Company, New York City, 8 June 1860, and 6 July 1860, Gibbs Letterpress.

[36]1848 Daybook, 118; 1862 Daybook, 1512; Gibbs Record Book, 20-25; Author unknown, "History of the First United Methodist Church of Huntsville," 1-19, W.S. Gibbs Collection, Huntsville, Texas.

[37]1848 Daybook, *passim*; 1862 Daybook, *passim*; D'Anne Crews, *Huntsville and Walker County, Texas*, 17-35.

[38]U. S. Bureau of the Census, "Slave Schedule," Walker County, Texas, 1850, 9; U. S. Bureau of the Census, "Slave Schedule," Walker County, Texas, 1860, 2; 1848 Daybook, *passim*; David R. Goldfield, *Cotton Fields and Skyscraper* (Baton Rouge: Louisiana State University Press, 1982), 81.

[39]D'Anne Crews, *Huntsville and Walker County, Texas*, 136.

[40]1860 Daybook, 442-457; 1862 Daybook, 1072-1134.

[41]1862 Daybook, 1402; Confederate States of America, Quartermaster Handbook belonging to Sandford St. John Gibbs; Author unknown, "The Smiths and Why They Came to Texas," 9, W.S. Gibbs Collection.

[42]1860 Daybook, 458; 1862 Daybook, 1127-1181.

[43]M.C. Rogers to President Andrew Johnson, 25 September 1865, Mae Wynne McFarland Collection, Archives, Sam Houston State University.

[44]Unpublished diary of Martha Ann Otey, Otey Collection, Thomason Room, Newton Gresham Library, Sam Houston State University.

[45]Otey diary, 1-10.

[46]M.A. Otey to her father, Edward Dromgoole Nolley, 22 March 1866, Otey Collection.

[47]M.A. Otey to her mother, Mary Frances Nolley, 25 April 1866, Otey Collection.

[48]M.A. Otey to Dr. and Mrs. LeGrand, 11 June 1866, Otey Collection.

[49]*Ibid.*

[50]*Ibid.*

[51]*Ibid.*

[52]M.A. Otey to her mother, Mary Frances Nolley, 29 June 1866, Otey Collection.

[53]M.A. Otey to Dr. and Mrs. LeGrand, 11 June 1866, Otey Collection.

[54]M.A. Otey to Mary Frances Nolley, 29 June 1866, Otey Collection; Thomas Jewett Goree to Eliza T. Nolley, 15 October 1867, Thomas Jewett Goree Papers, Thomason Room, Newton Gresham Library, Sam Houston State University.

[55]W.C. Nunn, *Texas Under the Carpetbaggers* (Austin: The University of Texas Press, 1962), 80-86.

[56]*Ibid.*

[57]*Ibid.*

[58]*Report on the Condition of the Texas State Penitentiary for the Years 1871-1872* (Austin: James P. Newcomb and Company, 1873), 3-7; D'Anne Crews, *Huntsville and Walker County, Texas,* 42 and 296-297.

[59]*Report on the Condition of the Texas State Penitentiary 1871-2*, 4-5.

[60]*Biennial Reports of the Commissioners, Superintendent, Financial Agent and Subordinate Officers of the Texas State Penitentiaries for the Fiscal Years ending August 31, 1907 and August 31, 1908* (Austin: Von Boeckmann-Jones Co., Printers, 1908), 12 and 31-32; *Biennial Reports of the Directors and Superintendent of the Texas State Penitentiary at Huntsville, Texas, with the Report of the Prison Physician, Commencing December 1, A.D. 1878, and Terminating October 31, A.D. 1880* (Galveston: News Book and Job Office, 1881), 51; *Biennial Report of the Superintendent of the Texas State Penitentiaries for Twenty-Four Months Ending August 31, 1910* (n. p.: n. p., 1910), 35.

[61]S. G. Reed, *A History of the Texas Railroads and of Transportation Conditions under Spain and Mexico and the Republic and the State* (Houston: St. Clair Publishing Company, 1941), 315-316.

[62]1860 Daybook, 738 and 796; Gibbs Inactive Land Book, Walker County, East J.J. Crowson Grant, Abstract Number 122, Certificate Number 319.

[63]Will of Thomas Gibbs, Vol. H., Probate Minutes, Walker County, Texas, 123 and 146-149.

[64]*Ibid.*, 248-264.

[65]*Ibid.*, Walker, *Penology for Profit*, 64-66.

[66]Will of Thomas Gibbs, 248-264.

[67]"The Smiths and Why They Came to Texas," 15-17; Deed from Thomas

Arthur Gibbs to Sandford St. John Gibbs, 23 February 1874, Gibbs vault.

[68]Walker, *Penology for Profit*, 84-86; Mae Wynne McFarland, "Penitentiary Notes," Archives, Sam Houston State University.

[69]Jack Humphries, "History of Sam Houston State University," 31. This is the draft of a proposed volume on the history of the university, W. S. Gibbs Collection.

[70]*Ibid.*, 33-35; D'Anne Crews, *History of Huntsville and Walker County, Texas*, 43.

[71]Bond of citizens of Huntsville to Governor O.M. Roberts to secure Sam Houston Normal Institute for Huntsville, 18 July 1879, W. S. Gibbs Collection; Sandford Gibbs *et al* to Governor O. M. Roberts, 21 May 1879, W. S. Gibbs Collection.

[72]"Gibbs Genealogy," W.S. Gibbs Collection.

Chapter II

[1]Will of Sandford St. John Gibbs, Volume K, Probate Minutes, Walker County, Texas, 585-588.

[2]Record of Inventory and Appraisement of the Property of Sandford St. John Gibbs, Book L, Probate Minutes, Walker County, Texas, 23-96; "Tax Receipts, Sundry Counties Beginning 1860-1899, Inclusive," Gibbs Brothers and Company.

[3]"The Smiths and Why They Came to Texas," 1-3.

[4]*Ibid.*, 3-4.

[5]*Ibid.*, 6-7.

[6]*Ibid.*

[7]*Ibid.*, 2-9.

[8]Interview with Luteola Gibbs Hawley by Wilbourn Sandford Gibbs, 26 October 1964, W. S. Gibbs Collection.

[9]Interview with Virginia Gibbs Smyth by the author, 6 November 1986.

[10]Miriam Gurko, *The Ladies of Seneca Falls: The Birth of the Woman's Rights Movement* (New York: Schocken, 1976), 171-190; Aileen S. Kraditor, *The Ideas of the Woman Suffrage Movement, 1890-1920* (New York: Norton, 1981), 75-122.

[11]Nancy Klugh Brown, "Thomas Clifton Gibbs," W. S. Gibbs Collection; Clarence R. Wharton, *Texas Under Many Flags* IV (Chicago: The American Historical Society, Inc., 1930), 65.

[12]Tom Randle interview by the author, 11 March 1986; for a discussion of the rights of landowners versus tenants as practiced in the late nineteenth-century South see Roger L. Ransom and Richard Sutch, *One Kind of Freedom: The Economic Consequences of Emancipation* (Cambridge: Cambridge University Press, 1977), 81-105.

[13]Walter L. Buenger and Joseph A. Pratt, *But Also Good Business: Texas Commerce Banks and the Financing of Houston and Texas, 1886-1986* (College Station: Texas A&M University Press), 1986, 12-18; Avery Luvere Carlson, *A Monetary and Banking History of Texas from the Mexican Regime to the Present Day, 1821-1929* (Fort Worth: The Fort Worth National Bank, 1930), 14-16.

[14]Atherton, *Southern Country Store*, 87-144; Larry Schweikart, *Banking in the American South from the Age of Jackson to Reconstruction* (Baton Rouge: Louisiana State University Press, 1987), 208-212.

[15]Lynne Pierson Doti and Larry Schweikart, *Banking in the American West from the Gold Rush to Deregulation* (Norman: Oklahoma University Press, 1991), 25-26.

[16]1847 Daybook, 443, 545, 570, and 573.

[17]1862 Daybook, 1344, 1407, and 1451; Kittrell, *The Kittrell Journal*, 93, 260 and 264.

[18]Joe E. Ericson, *Banks and Bankers in Early Texas, 1835-1875* (New Orleans: Polyanthos, 1976), 23 and 76; G.A. Wynne, "History of First National Dates Back to Early Days," *Huntsville Item*, 19 February 1940.

[19]Buenger and Pratt, *But Also Good Business*, 18-36.

[20]Joseph M. Grant and Lawrence L. Crum, *The Development of State Chartered Banking in Texas from Predecessor Systems until 1970* (Austin: Bureau of Business Research, University of Texas, 1978), 23-35.

[21]Wynne, "History of First National," *Huntsville Item*, 19 February 1940.

[22]Minutes of Meetings, Gibbs National Bank Board of Directors, 1-11, Archives of First National Bank, Huntsville, Texas.

[23]Marilyn McAdams Sibley, *George W. Brackenridge, Maverick Philanthropist* (Austin: University of Texas Press, 1973), 101.

[24]"Memorial Page to Mrs. Sallie E. Gibbs," Minutes of Meetings, Gibbs National Bank Board of Directors.

[25]Minutes of Meetings, Gibbs National Bank Board of Directors, 19 January 1901, 31 January 1903, 29 January 1906; Thomas and Sandford Gibbs to E.B. Nicholls, 8 November 1860, Gibbs Letterpress.

[26]*Ibid.*

[27]Wynne, "History of First National"; Minutes of Meetings, Gibbs National Bank Board of Directors, *passim.*

[28]Minutes of Meetings, Gibbs National Bank Board of Directors, *passim.*

[29]*Ibid.*

[30]W.S. Gibbs, "A Bit of Bank History," 1-3, W.S. Gibbs Collection.

[31]*Ibid.*

[32]Minutes of Meetings, Gibbs National Bank Board of Directors, 10 October 1907.

[33]Alwyn Barr, *Reconstruction to Reform: Texas Politics, 1876-1906* (Austin: University of Texas Press, 1971), 125-160; Carlson, *Monetary and Banking History of Texas*, 57-61; Wynne, "History of First National"; Grant and Crum, *Development of State Chartered Banking In Texas,* 37-44.

[34]Wilbourn Smith Gibbs, "Autobiography," W.S. Gibbs Collection.

[35]"Gibbs Geneology," W.S. Gibbs Collection; Virginia Gibbs Smyth interview with author, 6 November 1986; Sarah Alla Hawley Potter to author, June 1987. Kidd-Key College grew out of an earlier institution founded in 1866. It was taken over by the Methodist Episcopal Church, South in 1875 and, as described by one author, "was an outstanding southern school for women recognized throughout the Southwest for its programs." The school incurred heavy indebtedness during the 1920's and early 1930's and was turned over to its creditors, who closed it in 1935. Donald W. Whisenhunt, *The Encyclopedia of Texas Colleges and Universities: An Historical Profile* (Austin: Eakin Press, 1986), 69.

[36]Brown, "Thomas Clifton Gibbs"; Cecile Gibbs Gee, "The Story of Her Life," 3-5.

[37]"Gibbs Genealogy," W.S. Gibbs Collection; Virginia Gibbs Smyth interview with author, 6 November 1986; Sarah Alla Hawley Potter to author, June 1987.

[38]Buenger and Pratt, *But Also Good Business,* 33-34; Donald Cameron Gibbs, "Dr. James Philip Gibbs," W.S. Gibbs Collection; *The Texas Gulf Coast: Its History and Development* III (New York: The Lewis Historical Publishing Company, Inc., 1955), 391-392.

[39]"Gibbs Genealogy," W.S. Gibbs Collection; Luteola Gibbs Hawley interview with W.S. Gibbs, 26 October 1964; Sarah Alla Hawley Potter to author, June 1987.

[40]Virginia Gibbs Smyth interview with author, 26 November 1986.

[41]*Ibid.*; "Annual Report for 1905 by W.S. Gibbs to his mother, Mrs. Sallie E. Gibbs," W.S. Gibbs Collection.

[42]"Annual Report for 1905," W. S. Gibbs Collection.

[43]Charles Mohr, *The Timber Pines of the Southern United States*. U.S. Department of Agriculture, Division of Forestry Bulletin No. 18 (1897); S.B. Buckley, "Pine Lands of Southeastern Texas," *Texas Almanac 1868*, 92. Quoted in Robert Maxwell and Robert D. Baker, *Sawdust Empire: The Texas Lumber Industry 1830-1940* (College Station: Texas A&M Press, 1983), 3.

[44]Maxwell and Baker, *Sawdust Empire*, 3-4.

[45]*Ibid.*

[46]Easton, "History of the Texas Lumbering Industry," 54-73.

[47]Robert S. Maxwell, *Whistle in the Piney Woods: Paul Bremond and the Houston, East and West Texas Railway* (Texas Gulf Coast Historical Association, Volume VII, No. 2, 1963), 9-21; Maxwell and Baker, *Sawdust Empire*, 22-39.

[48]Fred Sellers interview with author, 6 October 1978. Sellars, now deceased, was a native East Texan and long-time manager of the commissary for the Boettcher Lumber Company in Huntsville, Texas.

[49]Maxwell and Baker, *Sawdust Empire*, 17-50; Ruth A. Allen, *East Texas Lumber Workers: An Economic and Social Picture, 1870-1950* (Austin: University of Texas Press, 1961), 180-181.

[50]Maxwell and Baker, *Sawdust Empire*, 22-31.

[51]*Ibid.*, 99-100; Mary Lasswell, *John Henry Kirby: Prince of the Pines* (Austin: Encino Press, 1967), 42-53.

[52]Maxwell and Baker, *Sawdust Empire*, 100-101; Lasswell, *John Henry Kirby*, 75-90.

[53]Allen, *East Texas Lumber Workers,* 180-181; Maxwell and Baker, *Sawdust Empire*, 104-105.

[54]Easton, "The Texas Lumbering Industry," ix and 101-110.

[55]Gibbs Inactive Land Book, Castro County; Walker County Tax Rolls, 1886-1914.

[56]Walker County Probate Minutes, Book M, 446-448; Book N, 1, 182 and 215.

[57]Gibbs Inactive Land Book, Newton County; Ruth Hansbro, "History of San Jacinto County," M.A. thesis, Sam Houston State Teachers College, 1940, 76-82; A. C. Ford to W. S. Gibbs, 4 April 1907. Letter is reprinted in volume 2 of the Defendant's Exhibits, *Gibbs Brothers v. Palmetto Lumber Co.*, Gibbs Brothers and Company.

[58]Gibbs Inactive Land Book, Newton County; Hansbro, "History of San Jacinto County," 76-82; Walker County Tax Rolls, 1900-1920; A.C. Ford to W.

L. E. O'Brien, 28 March 1924, Volume 2 of Defendant's Exhibits, *Gibbs Brothers and Company v. Palmetto Lumber Co.,* Gibbs Brothers and Company.

[59]Unattributed obituary of Sallie E. Gibbs, W. S. Gibbs Collection. Additional evidence that the "bundle of sticks" story may not have been unique to the Gibbses but rather appeared as a tale commonly featured in accounts of other legendary family businesses can be found in Cass Warner Sperling and Cork Millner with Jack Warner, Jr., *Hollywood Be Thy Name: The Warner Brothers Story* (Rocklin, California: Prima Publishing, 1994), 2.

Chapter III:

[1]Partnership Agreement, 30 December 1916, Gibbs Brothers and Company, W.S. Gibbs Collection.

[2]*Ibid.*

[3]*Ibid.*

[4]*Ibid.*

[5]Deed from Sallie E. Gibbs to W.S. Gibbs *et al*, Big Deeds Drawer, Gibbs Brothers and Company; Active Land Book and Inactive Land Book, Gibbs Brothers and Company.

[6]Affidavit by J. William Oliphint certifying his association with Gibbs Brothers and Company for purposes of proving company ownership of certain lands in the Simon Sanchez League in Henderson County, Texas, 19 March 1934.

[7]Interview with Tom Randle, 4 February 1987; Interview with Ed Sandhop, Jr., 4 February 1987.

[8]Donald Cameron Gibbs, "Dr. J. Philip Gibbs," W. S. Gibbs Collection; Interview with Virginia Gibbs Smyth, 6 November 1986.

[9]Interview with Virginia Gibbs Smyth, 6 November 1986.

[10]Inactive Land Book, Castro County, Gibbs Brothers and Company.

[11]Land and Team Book, 1917-1958, *passim.*

[12]David A. Shannon, *Twentieth Century America: The Twenties and Thirties* (Chicago: Rand McNally College Publishing Company, 1977), 70-75.

[13]Seth S. McKay and Odie B. Faulk, *Texas After Spindletop* (Austin: Steck-Vaughn Company, 1965), 98-99.

[14]*Ibid.*, 99-104.

[15]Wharton, *Texas Under Many Flags*, 65; Virginia Gibbs Smyth interview

with author, 6 November 1986.

[16]Brown, "Thomas Clifton Gibbs," 1-2. Walker County Genealogical Society and Walker County Historical Commission, *Walker County, Texas: A History* (Dallas: Curtis Media Corporation, 1986), 55.

[17]Letter from W. S. Gibbs to Ms. Fannie Lee Sparks, South Carolina, 28 January 1969, W. S. Gibbs Collection.

[18]*Huntsville Item*, 11 March 1920.

[19]*Ibid.*; Logan Wilson, "A Sociological Study of Huntsville, Texas," (M.A. thesis, University of Texas, 1927), 51.

[20]"Certified Copy of Resolution for Change of Name, The Gibbs National Bank, Huntsville, Texas, 9 January 1923," W.S. Gibbs Collection.

[21]*Huntsville Item,* 18 February 1926, and 7 January 1926.

[22]W.S. Gibbs, "Brief History of Huntsville First National Bank," 1982, W.S. Gibbs Collection.

[23]Brown, "Thomas Clifton Gibbs," 1-2; Unattributed obituaries of Thomas Clifton Gibbs, W.S. Gibbs Collection.

[24]Shannon, *Twentieth Century America*, 73-74; Dumas Malone and Basil Rauch, *War and Troubled Peace, 1917-1939* (New York: Appleton-Century-Crofts, 1960), 123-125; William E. Leuchtenburg, *The Perils of Prosperity, 1914-1932* (Chicago: University of Chicago Press, 1958), 178-188.

[25]Inactive Land Book, Montgomery County, Gibbs Brothers and Company.

[26]Land and Team Book, 1917-1958, 33-137; Farm lease contract, 1920's, Gibbs Brothers and Company.

[27]Farm lease contracts, 1920's, Gibbs Brothers and Company.

[28]Pasture leases with R.B. Stutts and R.E. Samuel, 1954, Gibbs Brothers and Company.

[29]*Ibid.*

[30]Land and Team Book, 1917-1958, 33-137.

[31]McKay and Faulk, *Texas After Spindletop,* 117-127; Lionel V. Patenaude, *Texans, Politics and the New Deal* (New York: Garland Publishing, Inc., 1983), 1-8; Donald W. Whisenhunt, *The Depression in Texas: The Hoover Years* (New York: Garland Publishing, Inc., 1983), 22-71.

[32]Land and Team Book, 1917-1958, 138-247.

[33]Gavin Wright, *Old South, New South: Revolutions in the Southern Economy Since the Civil War* (New York: Basic Books, Inc., 1986), 226-235; William C. Holley, Ellen Winston, and T.J. Woofter, Jr., *The Plantation South: 1934-1937* (Washington: Works Progress Administration, Divison of Social

Research, Research Monograph XXII, 1940; reprint, New York: DaCapo Press, 1971), xi-22 (page citations are to the reprint editon); T.J. Woofter, with the collaboration of Gordon Blackwell, Harold Hoffsommer, James W. Maddox, Jean M. Massell, B.O. Williams, and Waller Wynne, Jr., *Landlord and Tenant on the Cotton Plantation* (Washington: Works Progress Administration, Division of Social Research, Research Monograph V, 1936; reprint, New York: DaCapo Press, 1971), 41-47 and 145-189; Charles S. Johnson, Edwin R. Embree, and W.W. Alexander, *The Collapse of Cotton Tenancy: Summary of Field Studies and Statistical Surveys, 1933-1935* (Chapel Hill: University of North Carolina Press, 1935), 41-45.

[34]James William Martin, "History of Forest Conservation in Texas, 1900-1935" (M.A. thesis, Stephen F. Austin State College, 1966), 6.

[35]W. Goodrich Jones to *Daily Press of Texas*, 23 December 1918, reproduced in Martin, "History of Forest Conservation in Texas," 172.

[36]John A. Haislet, "Texans Evolve a State Forestry Agency," *Texas Forestry* V (May 1964), 6-7.

[37]W.L. (Bill) Carroll interview with author, 4 February 1987.

[38]*Ibid.*

[39]Deed from Gibbs Brothers and Company to Messrs. Morgan, Lindsey and Lindsey, Big Deeds Drawer, Gibbs Brothers and Company.

[40]Deed from Gibbs Brothers and Company to Weir Longleaf Lumber Company, Big Deeds Drawer, Gibbs Brothers and Company.

[41]Inactive Land Book, Madison County, Gibbs Brothers and Company.

[42]Maxwell and Baker, *Sawdust Empire,* 208-209.

[43]Easton, "History of the Texas Lumbering Industry," 437-438.

[44]Deed from Gibbs Brothers and Company to the United States Government, Big Deeds Drawer, Gibbs Brothers and Company; Maxwell and Baker, *Sawdust Empire*, 208-209. Maxwell and Baker, in their discussion of the establishment of the national forests in Texas, identify Gibbs Brothers incorrectly as a lumber company. In point of fact, the Gibbses never engaged in lumbering, even though they owned vast stands of timber and frequently entered into long-term contracts with lumber companies that wished to harvest and process the trees. Gibbs Brothers only grew the timber; they never attempted the milling, finishing, or retail sale of the lumber itself.

[45]Deed from Gibbs Brothers and Company to the United States Government, Big Deeds Drawer, Gibbs Brothers and Company.

[46]Gibbs, "Gibbs Genealogy," W.S. Gibbs Collection; Virginia Gibbs Smyth interview with author, 6 November 1986.

[47]Patenaude, *Texans: Politics and the New Deal*, 160-167; McKay and Faulk, *Texas After Spindletop*, 117-181.

Afterword:

[1]Gibbs, "Gibbs Genealogy," W. S. Gibbs Collection.

[2]Paul Port and P. Allan Port, "Brief History of the Company," W.S. Gibbs Collection.

[3]Paul Port to Dr. J. Philip Gibbs, 14 July 1949, W. S. Gibbs Collection.

[4]"Gibbs Brothers and Company, Supplemental Agreement, 1 October 1961," W.S. Gibbs Collection.

[5]Charles Dwyer, director, Thomason Rare Books Room, Newton Gresham Library, Sam Houston State University, interview with author, 4 April 1985.

[6]Blaine A. Brownell, *The Urban Ethos in the South: 1920-1930* (Baton Rouge: Louisiana State University Press, 1975), xx-xxi, 40-48, 117, and 168; Carl V. Harris, *Political Power in Birmingham 1871-1921* (Knoxville: University of Tennessee Press, 1977), 271-272; Char Miller and Heywood T. Sanders, *Urban Texas: Politics and Development* (College Station: Texas A&M University Press, 1990), 3-29; Christine Meisner Rosen, "The Power of Business Elites in the History of the City," *Reviews In American History* 15 (June 1987), 301-307; George B. Tindall, "Business Progressivism: Southern Politics in the Twenties," *The South Atlantic Quarterly* LXII (1963), 92-106; Dewey W. Grantham, *Southern Progressivism: The Reconciliation of Progress and Tradition* (Knoxville: University of Tennessee Press, 1983), 275-318.

[7]Brownell, *Urban Ethos in the South,* 117 and 168.

[8]Edward C. Fritz, *Sterile Forest: The Case Against Clearcutting* (Austin: Eakin Press, 1983), xi; Edward C. Fritz, *Clearcutting: A Crime Against Nature* (Austin: Eakin Press, 1989), xx.

[9]Contract between Gibbs Brothers and Company and Georgia-Pacific (Louisiana-Pacific), Gibbs Brothers and Company; Mary Vick Rainey interview with author, 1 June 1987.

[10]Interview by the author with George Beto, 11 March 1986.

Selected Bibliography

Manuscript Materials:

Deed Records. Walker County, Texas. Walker County Courthouse, Huntsville, Texas.

Probate Records. Walker County, Texas. Walker County Courthouse, Huntsville, Texas.

Tax Rolls. Grimes County, Texas. Grimes County Courthouse, Anderson, Texas.

Tax Rolls. San Jacinto County, Texas. San Jacinto County Courthouse, Coldspring, Texas.

Tax Rolls. Walker County, Texas. Walker County Courthouse, Huntsville, Texas.

United States Government. Bureau of the Census. "Slave Schedule, 1850," Walker County, Texas. Archives Division, Texas State Library, Austin, Texas.

United States Government. Bureau of the Census. "Slave Schedule, 1860," Walker County, Texas. Archives Division, Texas State Library, Austin, Texas.

The following materials are housed in the vault at Gibbs Brothers and Company, Huntsville, Texas:

Accounts Ledger, 1852.

Accounts Ledger, 1860.

Active Land Books.

Contract and agreements, assorted, between Gibbs Brothers and Company and other firms.

Daybook, 1841.

Daybook, 1846.

Daybook, 1847.

Daybook, 1858.

Daybook, 1862.

Daybook, 1866.

Deed Records.

Defendant's Exhibits, *Gibbs Brothers and Company v. Palmetto Lumber Company.*

Inactive Land Books.

Land and Team Book, 1917-1958.

Land and Team Book, 1958 to present.

Land Use Contracts.

Letterpress, 1859.

Minerals Only Books.

Partnership Agreement, 30 December 1916, Gibbs Brothers and Company.
Records, 1861.
Supplemental Partnership Agreement, 1 October 1961.
Tax Receipts. Sundry Counties, 1860-1899.

The following material has been gathered together to form the W.S. (Wilbourn Sandford) Gibbs Collection. Much of the collecting was done by Mr. Gibbs himself. It is housed in a four-drawer filing cabinet at Gibbs Brothers and Company:

Author unknown. "History of the First Methodist Church of Huntsville."
Author unknown. "The Smiths and Why They Came to Texas." (This appears to have been written by W.S. Gibbs from notes of an interview with Luteola Gibbs Hawley.)
"Bond of Citizens of Huntsville to Governor O.M. Roberts to secure the Sam Houston Normal Institute for Huntsville, July 18 1879."
Brown, Nancy Klugh. "Thomas Clifton Gibbs."
Gee, Cecile Gibbs. "The Story of Her Life."
Gee, Judge Thomas Gibbs. "Sandford St. John Gibbs."
Gibbs, Donald Cameron. "Dr. J. Philip Gibbs."
Gibbs, Wilbourn Sandford. "Brief History of Huntsville First National Bank."
______. "Genealogy of the Descendants of Hiram Gibbs."
Gibbs, Wilbourn Smith. "A Bit of Bank History."
______. "Annual Report for 1905 by W.S. Gibbs to his Mother, Sallie E. Gibbs."
______. "Autobiography."
Humphries, Jack. "History of Sam Houston State University." Draft of three chapters of a proposed history of the school.
Obituary of Sallie E. Gibbs.
Obituary of Thomas Clifton Gibbs.

The following materials are housed in the Archives, Sam Houston State University, Huntsville, Texas:

MacFarland, Mae Wynne. Papers.
______. "Penitentiary Notes."

The following materials are housed in the Thomason Room, Newton Gresham Library, Sam Houston State University, Huntsville, Texas:

Goree, Thomas Jewett. Papers.
Otey, Martha Anne. Papers.

The following materials are housed in the files of First National Bank, Huntsville, Texas:

Daily Ledgers. Gibbs National Bank, 1890-1922.
Minutes of Meetings of the Board of Directors. Gibbs National Bank, 1890-1922.

Books:

Allen, Ruth. *East Texas Lumber Workers: An Economic and Social Picture, 1870-1950.* Austin: University of Texas Press, 1961.

Atherton, Lewis E. *The Southern Country Store, 1800-1860.* Baton Rouge: Louisiana State University Press, 1949.

Barker, Eugene C. *The Life of Stephen F. Austin, Founder of Texas, 1793-1836.* N.P.: Lamar and Barton, Cokesbury Press, 1926. Reprint, Austin: University of Texas Press, 1969.

Barr, Alwyn. *Reconstruction to Reform: Texas Politics, 1876-1906.* Austin: University of Texas Press, 1971.

Barrett, John W., ed. *Regional Silviculture of the United States.* Second Edition. New York: John Wiley & Sons, 1980.

Biennial Reports of the Commissioners, Superintendent, Financial Agent and Subordinate Officers of the Texas State Penitentiaries for the Fiscal Years ending August 31, 1907 and August 31, 1908. Austin: Von Boeckmann-Jones Co., Printers, 1908.

Biennial Reports of the Directors and Superintendent of the Texas State Penitentiary at Huntsville, Texas, with the Report of the Prison Physician, Commencing December 1, A.D. 1878, and Terminating October 31, A.D. 1880. Galveston: News Book and Job Office, 1881.

Biennial Report of the Superintendent of the Texas State Penitentiaries for Twenty-four Months Ending August 31, 1910. N.P.: N.P., 1910.

Binkley, William C. *The Texas Revolution.* Baton Rouge: Louisiana State University Press, 1952.

Brownell, Blaine A. *The Urban Ethos in the South, 1920-1930.* Baton Rouge: Louisiana State University Press, 1975.

Buenger, Walter L. and Joseph A. Pratt. *But Also Good Business: Texas Commerce Banks and the Financing of Houston and Texas, 1886-1986.* College Station: Texas A&M Press, 1986.

Carlson, Avery Luvere. *A Monetary and Banking History of Texas from the Mexican Regime to the Present Day, 1821-1929.* Fort Worth: The Fort Worth National Bank, 1930.

Clark, Thomas D. *The Greening of the South: The Recovery of Land and Forest.* Lexington: The University Press of Kentucky, 1984.

______. *Pills, Petticoats and Plows: The Southern Country Store.* New York: Bobbs-Merrill Company, 1944.

Cox, Mrs. Davis. *Historic Huntsville Texas. Its Growth and Progress for Sixty-two Years, from 1837 to 1899.* N.P.: N.P., 1899.

Crews, D'Anne McAdams, ed. *Huntsville and Walker County, Texas: A Bicentennial History.* Huntsville: Sam Houston State University Press, 1976.

Doti, Lynne Pierson and Larry Schweikart. *Banking in the American West from the Gold Rush to Deregulation.* Norman: Oklahoma University Press, 1991.

Ericson, Joe E. *Banks and Bankers in Early Texas, 1835-1875.* New Orleans: Polyanthos, 1976.

Friend, Llerena. *Sam Houston: The Great Designer.* N.P.: Llerena Friend, 1954. Reprint, Austin: University of Texas Press, 1969.

Fritz, Edward C. *Clearcutting: A Crime Against Nature.* Austin: Eakin Press, 1989.

______. *Sterile Forest: The Case Against Clearcutting.* Austin: Eakin Press, 1983.

Goldfield, David R. *Cotton Fields and Skyscrapers.* Baton Rouge: Louisiana State University Press, 1982.

Grant, Joseph M. and Lawrence L. Crum. *The Development of State Chartered Banking in Texas from Predecessor Systems until 1970.* Austin: University of Texas Bureau of Business Research, 1978.

Grantham, Dewey W. *Southern Progressivism: The Reconciliation of Progress and Tradition.* Knoxville: University of Tennessee Press, 1983.

Gurko, Miriam. *The Ladies of Seneca Falls: The Birth of the Woman's Rights Movement.* New York: Schocken Books, 1976.

Harris, Carl V. *Political Power in Birmingham, 1871-1921.* Knoxville: University of Tennessee Press, 1977.

Holley, Mary Austin. *Texas.* Austin: The Texas State Historical Association, 1985.

Holley, William C., Ellen Winston, and T.J. Woofter, Jr. *The Plantation South, 1934-1937.* Washington: Works Projects Administration, Division of Social Research, Research Monograph XXII, 1940. Reprint, New York: DaCapo Press, 1971.

Houstoun, Mrs. E.M. (Matilda Charlotte). *Texas and the Gulf of Mexico: Or, Yachting in the New World.* Philadelphia: G.B. Zieber & Co., 1845. Reprint, Austin: Steck-Warlick Company, 1968.

Hyman, Harold. *Oleander Odyssey: The Kempners of Galveston, Texas, 1854-1980's.* College Station: Texas A&M University Press, 1990.

Johnson, Charles S., Edwin R. Embree and W. W. Alexander. *The Collapse of Cotton Tenancy: Summary of Field Studies and Statistical Surveys, 1933-1935.* Chapel Hill: University of North Carolina Press, 1935.

Jones, Fred Mitchell. *Middlemen in the Domestic Trade of the United States, 1800-1860.* Urbana: University of Illinois Press, 1937.

Kittrell, Pleasant Williams. *The Kittrell Journal.* Bryan, Texas: Family History Foundation, 1980.

Kraditor, Eileen. *The Ideas of the Woman Suffrage Movement, 1890-1920.* New York: W.W. Norton and Company, 1981.

Lack, Paul D. *The Texas Revolutionary Experience: A Political and Social History, 1835-1836.* College Station: Texas A&M University Press, 1992.

Lasswell, Mary. *John Henry Kirby: Prince of the Pines.* Austin: Encino Press, 1967.

Lazarou, Kathleen Elizabeth. *Concealed Under Petticoats: Married Women's Property and the Law of Texas, 1840-1913.* New York: Garland Publishing, Inc., 1986.

Leuchtenburg, William E. *The Perils of Prosperity, 1914-1932.* Chicago: University of Chicago Press, 1958.

Mabry, Mannie Lee, ed. *Union County Heritage, 1981.* N.P.: Union County Heritage Committee, 1981.

Malone, Dumas and Basil Rauch. *War and Troubled Peace, 1917-1939.* New York: Appleton-Century-Crofts, 1960.

Maxwell, Robert and Robert Baker. *Sawdust Empire: The Texas Lumber Industry, 1830-1940.* College Station: Texas A&M Press, 1983.

Maxwell, Robert. *Whistle in the Piney Woods: Paul Bremond and the Houston, East and West Texas Railway.* Texas Gulf Coast Historical Association, Volume VII, No. 2, 1963.

McKay, Seth S. and Odie Faulk. *Texas After Spindletop.* Austin: Steck-Vaughn Company, 1965.

Miller, Char and Heywood T. Sanders, eds. *Urban Texas: Politics and Development.* College Station: Texas A&M University Press, 1990.

Mohr, Charles. *The Timber Pines of the Southern United States.* U.S. Department of Agriculture, Division of Forestry Bulletin No. 18, 1897.

Nunn, W. C. *Texas Under the Carpetbaggers.* Austin: University of Texas Press, 1962.

Olien, Roger M. and Diana Davids Olien. *Wildcatters: Texas Independent Oilmen.* Austin: *Texas Monthly* Press, 1984.

Olmsted, Frederick Law. *A Journey Through Texas, or A Saddle-Trip on the Southwestern Frontier.* Austin: University of Texas Press, 1978.

Patenaude, Lionel. *Texans, Politics and the New Deal.* New York: Garland Publishing, Inc., 1983.

Ransom, Roger L. and Richard Sutch. *One Kind of Freedom: The Economic Consequences of Emancipation.* Cambridge: Cambridge University Press, 1977.

Reed, S.G. *A History of the Texas Railroads and of Transportation Conditions under Spain and Mexico and the Republic and the State.* Houston: St.Clair Publishing Company, 1941.

Report on the Condition of the Texas State Penitentiary, for the Years 1871-1872. Austin: James P. Newcomb and Company, 1873.

Schweikart, Larry. *Banking in the American South from the Age of Jackson to Reconstruction.* Baton Rouge: Louisiana State University Press, 1987.

Shammas, Carole, Marylynn Salmon, and Michel Dahlin. *Inheritance in America from Colonial Times to the Present.* New Brunswick: Rutgers University Press, 1987.

Shannon, David A. *Twentieth Century America, Volume II: The Twenties and Thirties.* Chicago: Rand McNally College Company, 1977.

Sibley, Marilyn McAdams. *George W. Brackenridge, Maverick Philanthropist.* Austin: University of Texas Press, 1973.

Spratt, John Stricklin. *The Road to Spindletop: Economic Change in Texas, 1875-1901.* Austin: University of Texas Press, 1970.

The Texas Gulf Coast: Its History and Development, Volume III. New York: The Lewis Historical Publishing Company, Inc., 1955.

Thompson, Thomas. *The Ware Boys: The Story of a Texas Family Bank.* Canyon: Staked Plains Press, 1978.

Vigness, David M. *The Revolutionary Decades: The Saga of Texas, 1810-1836.* Austin: Steck-Vaughn Company, 1965.

Walker County Genealogical Society and Walker County Historical Commission. *Walker County, Texas: A History.* Dallas: Curtis Media Corporation, 1986.

Walker, Donald R. *Penology for Profit: A History of the Texas Prison System, 1867-1912.* College Station: Texas A&M University Press, 1988.

Walton, Gary M. and James F. Shepherd, eds. *Market Institutions and Economic Progress in the New South, 1865-1900. Essays Stimulated by One Kind of Freedom: The Economic Consequences of Emancipation.* New York: Academic Press, 1981.

Wharton, Clarence R. *Texas Under Many Flags.* Chicago: The American Historical Society, 1930.

Whisenhunt, Donald W. *The Depression In Texas: The Hoover Years.* New York: Garland Publishing, Inc., 1983.

______. *The Encyclopedia of Texas Colleges and Universities: An Historical Profile.* Austin: Eakin Press, 1986.

Woofter, T. J., Jr., with the collaboration of Gordon Blackwell, Harold Hoffsommer, James G. Maddox, Jean M. Massell, B.O. Williams, and Waller Wynne, Jr. *Landlord and Tenant on the Cotton Plantation.* Washington, D.C.: Works

Progress Administration, Division of Social Research, Research Monograph V, 1936. Reprint, New York: DaCapo Press, 1971.

Wright, Gavin. *Old South, New South: Revolutions in the Southern Economy Since the Civil War*. New York: Basic Books, Inc., Publishers, 1986.

Writer's Program of the Works Projects Administration. *Texas: A Guide to the Lone Star State*. American Guide Series. New York: Hastings House Publishers, 1940.

Newspapers

Huntsville Item, 1853 through 1985.

Houston Chronicle, 1941.

Interviews

Beto, George. Interview by author, 11 March 1986.

Carroll, W.L. (Bill). Interview by author, 4 February 1987.

Dwyer, Charles. Interview by author, 4 April 1985.

Rainey, Mary Vick. Interview by author, 1 June 1987.

Randle, Tom. Interviews by author, 11 March 1986 and 4 February 1987.

Sandhop, Edwin G., Jr. Interviews by author, 4 February and 17 June 1987.

Sellars, Fred and Bryant. Interview by author, 6 October 1978.

Smyth, Virginia Gibbs. Interview by author, 6 November 1986.

Articles

Atherton, Lewis. "Itinerant Merchandising in the Antebellum South." *Bulletin of the Business Historical Society* XIX (1945): 35-59.

______. "The Pioneer Merchant in Mid-America." *The University of Missouri Studies* XIV:2 (1 April 1939): 7-135.

Haislet, John A. "Texans Evolve a State Forestry Agency." *Texas Forestry* V (May 1964): 6-7.

Miller, Edmund. "A Financial History of Texas." *Bulletin of the University of Texas* No. 37, 1916: 9-430.

Rosen, Christine Meisner. "The Power of Business Elites in the History of the City." *Reviews in American History* XV (June 1987): 301-307.

Tindall, George B. "Business Progressivism: Southern Politics in the Twenties." *The South Atlantic Quarterly* LXII (1963): 92-106.

Theses and Dissertations

Baldwin, John W: "An Early History of Walker County, Texas." M.A. thesis, Sam Houston State Teachers College, 1957.

Easton, Hamilton Pratt. "A History of the Texas Lumbering Industry." Ph.D. dissertation, University of Texas, 1947.

Hansbro, Ruth. "History of San Jacinto County." M.A. thesis, Sam Houston State Teachers College, 1940.

Manselle, Adele. "A History of Trinity County." M.A. thesis, Sam Houston State Teachers College, 1941.

Martin, James W. "A History of Forest Conservation in Texas, 1900-1935." M.A. thesis, Stephen F. Austin State University, 1966.

Mills, Robert E. "Navigation of the Trinity River." M.A. thesis, Sam Houston State Teachers College, 1943.

White, E. V. and William E. Leonard. "Studies in Farm Tenancy in Texas." *Bulletin of the University of Texas* No. 21, 1915.

Wilson, Logan. "A Sociological Study of Huntsville, Texas." M.A. thesis, University of Texas, 1927.

Index

Photographs

Photograph Identification

Page 148: Thomas Gibbs

Page 149: Sandford St. John Gibbs

Page 150: Sallie Elizabeth Smith Gibbs

Page 151: Sallie Gibbs as a young girl

Page 152: Sandford and Sallie Gibbs, circa 1881, with (left to right) Alla, Lena (daughter of Sandford Gibbs and his first wife), Luteola (between her parents), Wilbourn Smith, Sandford, Thomas, and James Philip

Page 153: Wilbourn Smith Gibbs

Page 154: Mary Alla Gibbs Robinson

Page 155: Thomas Clifton Gibbs

Page 156: Sarah Sandford Gibbs Norsworthy

Page 157: James Philip Gibbs

Page 158: Luteola Gibbs Hawley

Page 159: Gibbs family Christmas picture, 1910. Back row, left to right: James Philip Gibbs, Thomas Clifton Gibbs, William Smith Gibbs, "Nannie," H. Y. Robinson, Oscar Norsworthy, Pauline Gibbs, H. H. Hawley. Middle row: Mary McAshan Gibbs, Jamesetta Hunt Gibbs, Anné Nugent Gibbs, Sallie Smith Gibbs (holding Sarah Elizabeth Gibbs), Alla Gibbs Robinson (arm around Herndon Yoakum Robinson), Sarah Sandford Gibbs Norsworthy, Luteola Gibbs Hawley (arm around Henry Hawley). Front row: Virginia Gibbs, Kathleen Gibbs, Wilbourn Sandford Gibbs, Edith Gibbs (seated), Wilbourn Thomas Robinson (seated), Cecile Gibbs (seated)

Page 160: Wedding of Sarah Sandford Gibbs to Oscar Norsworthy, 1910. Luteola Gibbs, seventh from left; Alla Gibbs, left of groom; James Philip Gibbs, right of bride; Wilbourn Smith Gibbs, sixth from right

Page 161: Store corner, circa 1905

Page 162: Front of second Gibbs store, circa 1928

GIBBS · BROS.& CO.
1116

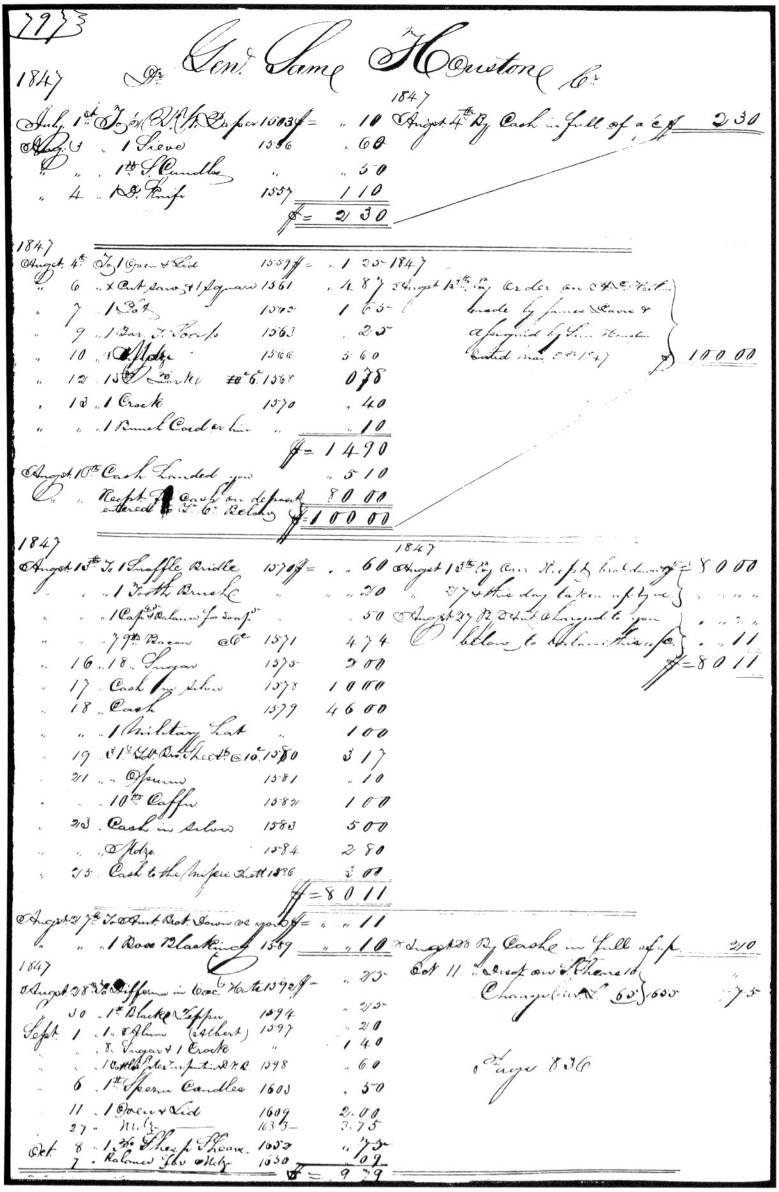

797

Dr. Genl. Sam Houston Cr.

1847

July 1st To 1/2 Qr. Wr. Paper 1503 $= .. 10 | 1847 August 4th By Cash in full of a/c $ 2 30
Aug. 3 .. 1 Sieve 1556 .. 60
" " .. 1lb S. Candles " .. 50
" 4 .. 1 D. Knife 1557 1 10
$= 2 30

1847

August 4th To 1 Oven & Lid 1559 $= .. 1 25 | 1847 August 12th By Order on C. H. & Co. ... made by James Davis & assigned by Sam Houston dated May 5th 1847 } $ 100 00
" 6 .. X Cut saw & 1 Square 1561 .. 4 87
" 7 .. 1 Pot 1562 1 65
" 9 .. 1 Bar S. Soap 1563 .. 25
" 10 .. Mdze 1566 5 60
" 12 .. 13lb ... #6 1568 0 78
" 13 .. 1 Crock 1570 .. 40
" " .. 1 Bunch Cord or line " .. 10
$= 14 90
August 10th Cash Loaned you .. 5 10
" " Recpt. for Cash on deposit entered to Yr. Cr. Below 80 00
$= 100 00

1847

August 13th To 1 Snaffle Bridle 1570 $= .. .. 60 | 1847 August 13th By Cash Recpt. ... $= 80 00
" " .. 1 Tooth Brush " .. .. 20 | " 27 & this day taken up by ... } .. .. ..
" " .. 1 Cap ... Balance for Soap .. 50 | August 27 By Amt. Charged to you below to balance this a/c } 11
" " .. 79lb Bacon @6c 1571 4 74 | $= 80 11
" 16 .. 18 .. Sugar 1575 2 00
" 17 .. Cash in Silver 1578 10 00
" 18 .. Cash 1579 46 00
" " .. 1 Military Hat " 1 00
" 19 .. 31 ... @10c 1580 3 17
" 21 .. Opium 1581 .. 10
" " .. 10lb Coffee 1582 1 00
" 23 .. Cash in Silver 1583 5 00
" " .. Mdze 1584 2 80
" 25 .. Cash to the Misses ... 1586 2 00
$= 80 11

August 27th To Amt. Brot. Down as you $= 11
" " .. 1 Box Blacking 1589 .. .. 10 | August 28 By Cash in full of a/c 2 10

1847 | Oct. 11 .. Disct. on ... Change ... 65} 1655 .. 75

August 28th To Difference in Exc. Note 1592 $= .. 25
" 30 .. 1lb Black Pepper 1594 .. 25
Sept. 1 .. 1 lb Alum (Albert) 1597 .. 20
" " .. 8 .. Sugar & 1 Crock " 1 40
" " .. 1 Cotton ... 1598 .. 60
" 6 .. 1lb Sperm Candles 1603 .. 50
" 11 .. 1 Oven & Lid 1609 2 00
" 27 .. Mdze 1633 3 75
Oct. 8 .. 1 pr. Sheep Shears 1652 .. 75
" 7 .. Balance ... Mdze 1650 .. 09
$= 9 79

Page 836

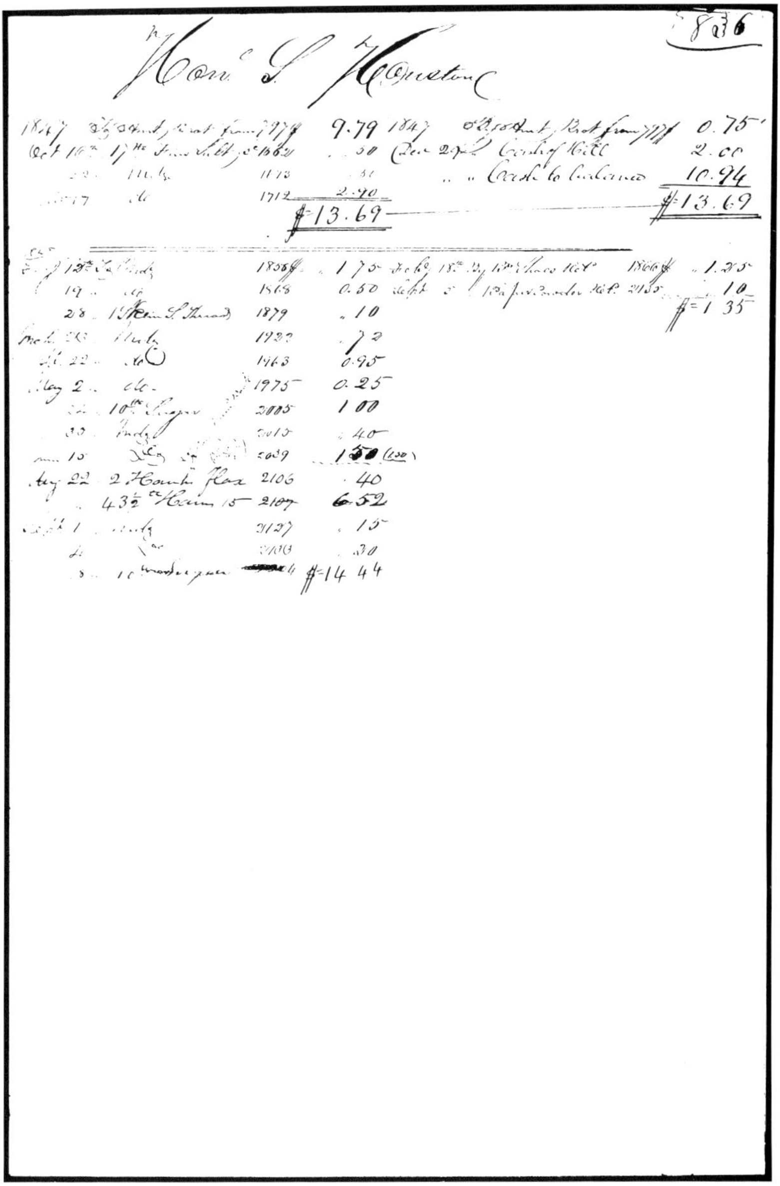

836

Hon. S. Houston

1847	[illegible] from	1779	9.79	1847	[illegible] from	1779	0.75
Oct 16th	1 [illegible]	1662	.50	Dec 29th	Cash of Hill		2.00
22	[illegible]	1173	.30		Cash to balance		10.94
27	do	1712	2.40				
			$13.69				$13.69

[illegible] 12th	[illegible]	1858	1.75	Feb 18th	By [illegible]	1866	1.25
19	do	1868	0.50	Sept 5	[illegible]	2135	.10
28	1 [illegible] Thread	1879	.10				$1.35
March 23	[illegible]	1922	.72				
April 22	do	1963	0.95				
May 2	do	1975	0.25				
22	10th Sugar	2005	1.00				
30	[illegible]	2015	.40				
June 15	[illegible]	2039	1.50 (1.50)				
Aug 22	2 Hanks Flax	2106	.40				
	43½ lb Ham 15	2107	6.52				
Sept 1	[illegible]	2127	.15				
4	[illegible]	2133	.30				
8	10 [illegible]	[illegible]	$14.44				

1873 - 1875

TELLER

WALKER
GIBBS
FIRST NATIONAL BANK

METHODIST CHURCH, HUNTSVILLE, TEXAS

Inside the Prison Walls
Huntsville, Texas
Picture taken 1873 or
1875

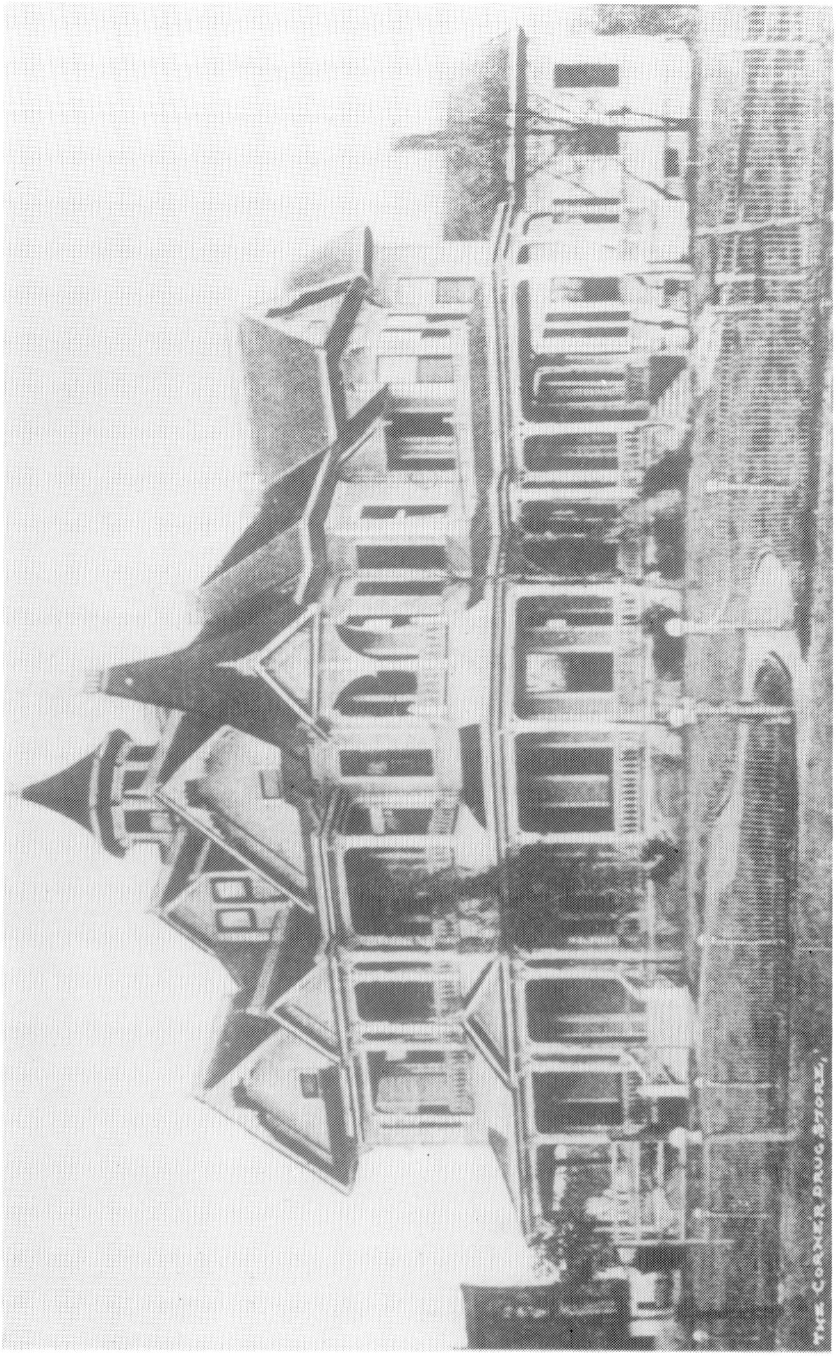
THE CORNER DRUG STORE.